Somebody's Watching Over Me

Dorothy and Joe H., early 1970s

Joe Wessels

Somebody's Watching Over Me

My Incredibly Blessed Life

by
Joe Wessels

Harrington Press
2007

©2007 by Joseph H. Wessels

This book may not be reproduced or distributed, in whole or in part, imprint or by any other means, without the written permission of the author or his family. Contact him at 2416 Bluestone Circle, Oshtemo, MI 49009.

Wessels, Joseph Henry, 1924–
   Somebody's watching over me : my incredibly blessed life. / by Joe Wessels. / Kalamazoo, Mich. : Harrington Press / 2007.
   xi, 164p. includes photos and index.
   1. Wessels, Joseph Henry, 1924– 2. Sales management—Michigan—biography 3. NuCon Systems (Kalamazoo, Mich.) 4. Industrial distributors—Michigan—Pneumatic equipment 5. Hydraulics—Equipment and supplies 6. Rose Arbor Hospice (Kalamazoo, Mich.) 7. Volunteer workers in terminal care—Kalamazoo County. 8. World War, 1939–1945—Cavalry operations. 9. Concentration camps—Austria—Ebensee 10. Movement for Spiritual Inner Awareness 11. Spiritual biography—Michigan I. Title
   921 .W515

ISBN: 978-0-9789126-4-2

Layout and book design by LanWord
Printed by Fidlar Doubleday Inc., Davenport, Iowa

Contents

Preface		ix
1	Early Years: 1924–1932	1
2	The Great Depression Begins: 1929–1931	11
3	Boyne City Years: 1936–1943	23
4	Working for Uncle Sam: 1943–1945	33
5	Crossing the Big Pond	43
6	Post-war jobs: Detroit, Michigan	65
7	Dorothy and Me	75
8	My Years at Ford Motor Company	83
9	Kalamazoo, Here We Come! 1959–present	91
10	Volunteering at Hospice	111
11	My Philosophy of Life	135
12	Looking Back	145
Index		157

Somebody's Watching Over Me

Preface

At the numerous requests of my beloved wife, Dorothy, I have decided to attempt to record my autobiography. I'm sure many people will find this to be kind of mundane and not very exciting because I am not a writer, but I do tell stories and I have many stories to tell.

My grandchildren always say, "Pop, tell us another story." Even my younger son, Steve, even when he was a kid, wanted to listen to family stories. Maybe it's genetics, his daughter also tells good stories:

You Were There

You were there to make me smile,
When I began to cry.
You helped me heal.
You are my guardian.

You were there to teach me how to
Play cards.
Everything from, go fish all the way to
    bridge.
You were my teacher.

You were there to guide me down
The right path when I was unsure which
Way to go.
You are my leader.

You were there to take me shopping
When I needed something new.
Anything from a new shirt to a new shoe.
You are my giver.

But all those things pushed aside,
You are . . .
You are my Pop.

— Amanda Wessels
March 10, 2006

Preface

Back in 2005, I began typing the manuscript for this book myself, and recently arranged with Brenda Fettig Murphy to edit them

I thank Brenda for her experience in book publishing and for the use of one of her drawings from *Living Well, Dying Well: Stories from Rose Arbor Hospice,* and also Laura Latiolais of Hospice Care of Southwest Michigan for releasing permission to include it here.

Joe Wessels
November 2007

Somebody's Watching Over Me

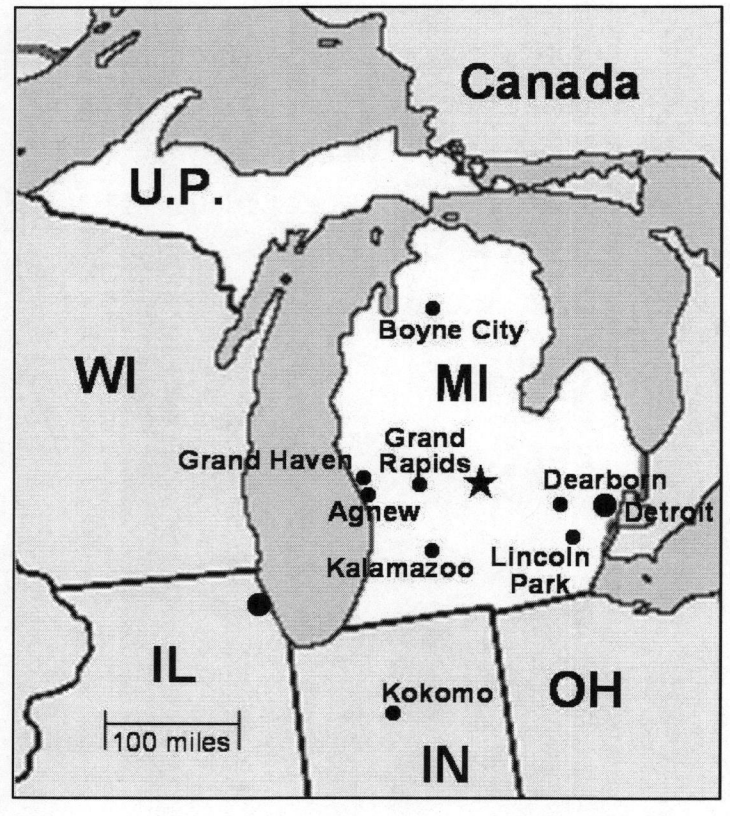

1

Early Years
1924 – 1932

I was born in Grand Haven, Michigan, at home on March 10, 1924. I was named after my grandfather, Joseph Henry Wessels. My mother was Emma Marie Bethke Wessels and my father was Joseph William Wessels.

My mother's parents lived on a farm in Agnew, which is located a few miles south of Grand Haven. Their names were Theodore and Augusta Bethke. Theodore was born of German parents who had migrated to the United States. Augusta was born in Germany and came to America where she met my grandfather. My grandparents had several children, many of whom died very young. The children who lived were my mother, her two sisters Marie and Ella, and one brother Walter. Of course, they have all died. Aunt Ella was my favorite.

When we were kids, my sister and I never received presents from our parents for birthdays or Christmas—nothing. My Aunt Ella's husband worked in a Kalamazoo paper mill, but when he was laid off, they both came to live in Boyne City with our family for a few months. I think it was a Christmas, after paper work started up again, that a big box arrived for us. In my box was a yellow dump truck and a little book of Christian prayers from Aunt Ella that I read over and over again.

Early Years

Great-grandmother Sarah Wessels was born in 1847 and died in 1925. My grandmother Wessels died during childbirth about 1903. My grandfather never remarried. My grandmother was of Spanish decent and my grandfather was Pennsylvania Dutch. My dad had a brother, Bert, and a sister, Ettie, who was several years older than my dad. My dad was born in 1901, and Ettie served as a mother to him. Bert married and had two sons, Glenn and Darwin. Ettie married and had two sons, Frank and Earl.

Shortly after my birth, my parents moved to Kokomo, Indiana, where my sister, Joy, was born in November 1927. After that, we moved to Lincoln Park, Michigan, where I attended kindergarten and first grade at Goodell School. My dad worked at a gas station. It was the beginning of the Great Depression, and there were a lot of unemployed people. He was held up three times by thugs from the Purple Gang. In 1931, he decided he had enough and moved us north to Boyne City.

My grandfather welcomed us in his home. For those days it was a comfortable home: a kitchen with a wood burning stove, two bedrooms, a living room with another wood burning stove, a dining room on the main floor with two bedrooms upstairs, and a root cellar below the kitchen. The house did not have electricity so we used kerosene lamps for lighting at night. Of course, we had no radio and no telephone. We had an outdoor toilet. This was the way we lived until I went into the army in March 1943.

Early Years

My dad and grandfather got jobs delivering coal from a large pile of coal located on the north side of Lake Charlevoix to a leather tannery located on the south side of the lake. It was hard work. They had to shovel the coal onto a truck, drive the truck to the tannery and shovel the coal off the truck. My dad was not very big and my grandfather was over sixty. The work was very strenuous for both of them, and they both suffered the consequences.

While my grandfather was alive, my sister and I got Christmas presents and had some pleasant memories. In the summer of 1932, an American Indian, who was a friend of my grandfather was visiting with him. He asked if I wanted a bow and arrow for Christmas. Naturally, I said yes.

The day before Christmas it snowed about a foot of snow. In 1932, I believe we had only one snow plow in town, so all the roads were blocked.

Christmas Eve came and went with no bow and arrow. On Christmas Day the snow continued to fall; the roads were impassable. Sometime in the afternoon, a knock sounded at the front door. It was my grandfather's friend, the American Indian. My grandfather greeted him and the Indian presented me with the bow and arrow. Of course, I was very happy to receive such a wonderful gift. It happened to be my last Christmas present until after I came home from overseas during World War II in 1945.

The significance of the gift became more appreciated many years after I matured. The Indian did not have transportation and the roads were impassable, so he walked from Walloon Lake about eight miles on snowshoes to give me the bow and arrow. Then, he had to walk back. He could have made many excuses not to keep his promise but he kept his word. He sure had integrity. I never saw him again, but he had a great impact on my life. He could have reasoned it was only an eight-year old kid, so why should I put all this effort in snow shoeing sixteen miles to take a bow and arrow to him? But he put himself to a great task to keep his word. I learned early in life the importance of doing what I say I am going to do. It is a reflection of my character, and determines whether or not I can be trusted.

There was a sheep pasture across the street. At the beginning of a blizzard, my dad and grandfather went to the pasture and saved several sheep that were trapped in snow drifts and carried them to their barn. They also saved a lamb whose mother had died in the storm. They brought the lamb to our house, made a pen for it, and put it in a room off the kitchen. We all took turns nursing it. The lamb happened to be a young buck, so we named him " Jake". In the spring we would take him into the yard where I played with him. Jake would instinctively try to butt me, but I would push his head down and jump out of his way. As he got bigger, we released him into the sheep pasture.

Early Years

Somebody's Watching Over Me

Lucky and Joe at 12, Boyne City, Michigan, in front of his grandfather.s house

2

The Great Depression Begins
1929 – 1931

In 1929 the Great Depression began. It was difficult for everybody. People did whatever they could do to survive. My grandfather was resourceful. He had two small buildings behind the house. One he converted into a small barn. He bought two cows, a Guernsey and a Jersey. We called them Molly and Daisy. My wonderful mother did the milking that provided us with fresh milk. She also put the milk into crocks. The cream would collect at the top. When enough cream was collected, she would put it into a churn where she made butter. I remember doing a lot of churning.

In the winter the cows were fed hay. When spring arrived, the grass started to grow. My parents would take the cows a couple blocks away to an open field, tie them with a tether so they could graze on fresh grass. In the evening we would bring the cows back to the barn.

One afternoon it started to storm with rain, lightening and thunder. My mother sent me to get the cows. I untied the ropes and started to walk the cows back to the barn. With the lightening and thunder, the cows got excited and started to run in order to get to the barn. One of the ropes got tangled around my leg, I fell down and the cow dragged me about one hundred yards back to the barn. I only had a few scratches and bruises, but my mother was so angry with the poor cow that she grabbed a broom and beat the cow around its head and behind.

The other building was made into a chicken coop. We had a hundred or more chickens. They provided us with fresh eggs and chicken to eat.

We always had at least an acre for a garden. In the spring, my grandfather would hire a man with a team of horses, who would plow the soil and drag it. Then we planted the seeds for the various crops: corn, carrots, potatoes, brown beans, peas, lettuce, radishes, tomatoes, etc. During the growing season, we all worked in the garden, hoeing and weeding. When the crops were grown, we harvested them. My mother would can a couple hundred quarts of vegetables where they were stored in our root cellar along with our potatoes. We also picked wild blackberries that were made into jam stored in our root cellar.

During the summer, our family did a variety of jobs working for farmers helping them to pick strawberries, raspberries and cherries. In the fall, we picked up potatoes. We did whatever we could do to earn a small amount of money. Like most kids growing up in the Depression, Joy and I didn't have much time for play.

Then, in 1933 my grandfather died. I can vividly recall coming home from a Buck Jones cowboy movie with my two buddies, Robert and Jim Sayles who lived down the street. Robert died many years ago, but Jim and I are still great friends [2005]. In the front of our house was a big black car (a hearse) that was there to get my grandfather. The undertaker brought the casket with my grandfather to our home where it was

The Great Depression Begins

placed in the living room for a couple of days for visitation by family members and friends.

As I recall, the undertaker charged my dad about $350 for funeral services. Of course, my dad didn't have the money, so he agreed to clear some wooded property during the summer to pay off the debt.

All summer long my mother would pack my dad and me a lunch. We would walk a few miles to the wooded property. My dad cut down the trees and trimmed them. My job was to pick up the branches and pile them. In July and August, it can get pretty hot in Boyne City, especially in the woods where there isn't much breeze and the insects are terrible. At nine years old, I would get tired in the afternoon.

One day I recall sitting on a stump and complaining to my dad that the bugs were stinging me. He merely said, "If you get off your ass and start piling brush, you won't notice them." I didn't get much sympathy.

In the summer of 1933 after my grandfather died, Aunt Ettie and my two cousins, Frank and Earl, came to see us. My cousins were both older than I was. She wanted some pictures and a couple pieces of furniture that belonged to my grandfather. Frank was a nice guy, but Earl was a bully and always pushing me around. So, I decided to get even with Earl. I took him to the sheep pasture and called for Jake.

Jake came running to us. He immediately chased us. Earl got scared and climbed a pole. Jake tried to butt me but I merely pushed on the top of his head, jumped aside and ran away, leaving Earl stranded. An hour or so later, Earl came back to the house. I never had any more problems with Earl.

The Great Depression Begins

For awhile, we were on welfare. I can remember my mother taking me to see the welfare agent to get script money that she used to buy shoes for me to go to school. It was difficult for her to ask for this kind of help. All the kids in town whose parents were on welfare were given the same kind of sweaters and jackets. I refused to wear them. I would wear hand-me-downs from a neighbor kid who was a couple of years older.

One night, I was sent to get a gallon of kerosene for our lamps. It was cold outside and about a mile roundtrip. I absolutely refused to dress in the welfare clothes. My parents sent me to my room until I agreed to wear the welfare clothes. When I finally realized it was dark outside so nobody would notice me, I agreed to wear the clothes.

President Roosevelt was elected and created government-sponsored work programs for unemployed workers. My dad worked for a short while for the Public Works Administration, receiving $40 per month, and my mother worked as a cook in restaurants and hotels.

When I was in either the fourth or fifth grade, after Christmas, the teacher went around the class and asked what each of us got for Christmas. I had not received any present. I was seated in the middle of the class and the kids before me were telling the teacher about their wonderful gifts. I was embarrassed to say that I did not receive any presents so I lied and told the teacher I had received skates, a sled and other gifts. I guess I made up my mind in my early childhood that if I ever had children, I would always be a good provider.

Sometime in the summer of 1936, my dad got a job in a tannery in Grand Haven. He sent money home to my mother periodically. One time

The Great Depression Begins

a few weeks went by and we were running low on food and money. My mother decided to write my dad and ask for some money. At that time a postage stamp cost three cents. Well, my poor mother found two cents. She looked through every cupboard and drawer, but was unable to find another penny so she could not send a letter to my dad. She was very desperate. Earlier they had sold the cows and chickens, and were not growing a garden, so my mother fed us cornmeal mush for a few days. Fortunately, my dad came home and we ate regular food again. I never forgot how important a penny can be.

Sometime before I started the seventh grade, we left Boyne City and moved to Grand Haven. My dad had a friend who owned a Ford coupe and drove us to Grand Haven. My mother and sister rode in the front seat and my dad and I rode in the trunk. It was cold and we were bundled in blankets. Every couple of hours the driver stopped, and we got out of the trunk to stretch. It was a difficult trip.

For a short while we stayed with my mother's parents. It was the first time I had seen my grandparents since I was born. They seemed nice enough, but they sure were miserly people. They never sent Joy or me a birthday card, Christmas card or gifts of any kind. They never bought us a five-cent ice cream cone; they were very tight. We moved into a rental place my parents found in town. My dad worked in a tannery, and my mother got a job as a seamstress in a factory that made gloves.

Being in Grand Haven was the happiest period of my childhood. The tannery had a gym that could be used by the employees and their families. Quite often I would go to the gym after school and play basketball.

When I first enrolled in school, the teacher introduced me to my first class. She asked the boy behind me to show me to my other classes. I asked him for his name and he said, "Jack Wessel, and my brother, Jim, is over there, and our cousin, Ed, is over there." So, there I was, a Wessels, with three Wessel boys in the same class. The teachers had a great time kidding us about our names. I don't know if we were distant relatives because my great-grandmother, Sarah, had thirteen children. Maybe some of them dropped the "s" off their name. Possibly we were distant cousins, but I never found out for sure.

After I finished the seventh grade, my parents bought me a beautiful red bicycle. It was the best gift I ever received as a child. Grand Haven is located on Lake Michigan with a beautiful beach called the Oval. I would often bike to the Oval for a swim.

Somebody's Watching Over Me

Pre-war jobs

3

Boyne City Years
1936 – 1943

During the middle of eighth grade, my dad had a heart attack so we moved back to Boyne City. He was confined to bed for weeks. My mother went to work again as a cook in restaurants.

Shortly after finishing the eighth grade, there was a bike race in Boyne City for boys up to 16 years old. It was about three miles long, and I happened to win the race. It was a thrill: I won a couple dollars and took my buddies, Jim and Rob, to the ice cream parlor for sodas.

Early that summer, I rode my bike to Walloon Lake Country Club to get a job as a caddy. The trip was about 22 miles roundtrip. I got the job. Thereafter I hitchhiked, and it was always easy to get a ride.

As a caddy, we were paid seventy-five cents for 18 holes and, if we were lucky, we got a twenty-five cent tip. I saved all my money in a jar that I kept under my bed. I never spent even a nickel for an ice cream cone. During the summer, I earned about $75 that I gave to my mother. She used the money to buy clothes for my sister and me for school, and also bought some coal for the winter.

After the caddy season, I got a job delivering the local paper, called the *Boyne Citizen*. As I

Boyne City Years

recall, I earned $6 a month plus received a fifteen-cent movie ticket. During the fall and spring months I rode my bike, but during the winter I walked the route which was about four miles. It wasn't fun, but it did keep me in good shape.

This was my program for the eighth, ninth and tenth grades: caddy in the summer, and do the newspaper route during the fall, winter and spring. When I was in the eleventh grade, I managed to get some other jobs. Boyne City did not have snow removal equipment, so occasionally I managed to get a job shoveling snow from the downtown streets into a dump truck. Most of the workers were men, while I was the only kid.

In May I got a job mowing lawns in the cemetery. The first day my boss said my mower was not cutting the lawn properly, so he tightened the blade and made it almost impossible to push the mower. Actually, I was going too fast and my boss wanted to make the job last longer. The next morning, I took a screw driver with me to work and secretly adjusted the blade which made it easier to push my mower, but I also slowed down. We also dug graves for newly deceased and filled them in. After Memorial Day, I got a job painting parking places on the streets. Again, my new boss was slow, to make the job last longer. Before caddy season started my buddy, Jim Sayles, and I got jobs working for a farmer picking up hay from the fields and storing the hay in the barn. We were paid $1 a day plus fed a large lunch of fried chicken and strawberry shortcake. It sure was hard work.

Walloon Lake Country Club had a grill that had three slot machines: dime, quarter and half dollar. One morning the caretaker, while opening the grill, was slugged by someone who wanted to steal the money from the slot machines. The assailant fled, and the caretaker was taken to the hospital. The golf pro offered me the job as night watchman for $30 a month. I slept in the grill on a cot. After everybody left for the day, I would lock up the grill, push the tables under the windows and pile the chairs on top of the tables. I thought if anyone should break a window and knock over a chair, I would awaken and be able to defend myself. My dad made me a blackjack from a piece of rubber hose and loaded it with buckshot. It was an effective weapon. I let all the caddies see it so they could tell their friends to discourage them from attempting to break in. I never had any trouble.

In addition to my pay of $30 per month, I had the choice of the first caddy job in the morning. Naturally, I always selected a golfer who tipped a quarter. Sometimes I got two jobs a day. Every few days, I would hitchhike home to see my parents. My mother would give me a bag full of sandwiches and some fruit, and I would return to the golf course.

When I entered the ninth grade, one of the classes I took was algebra. At first I had a lot of trouble with the concepts and got a C for my first card-marking. Then I found out that Jim's dad, Mr. Sayles, liked math and was very patient and helpful. So every night after my paper route, I would go with my algebra book to see Mr. Sayles who lived about a block from our house. I went from a C to an A in one card-marking.

When I got into the tenth grade, I had trouble with geometry. Again, Mr. Sayles helped me to grasp the concepts and I received an A in the class. I got straight A's in algebra and geometry thereafter. I was fortunate to learn early in life to ask for help if I didn't understand something.

Otherwise, I wouldn't learn. False pride can be a serious drawback.

After the golf season, I started my senior year in high school. In September I got a job at the Dilworth Hotel as a bellhop that I did after school. A couple weeks later, the night clerk became ill and was unable to work, and I was offered the job. It paid $10 a week. I worked seven nights a week from nine p.m. until seven a.m. During the night I would get a little rest by sleeping on the couch in the lobby. Then, of course, I went to school during the day. After class, I would hurry home so I could get a little more sleep.

One benefit from having this job was it provided me with plenty of time to study after the guests arrived in the evening. At home we had kerosene lamps, but in the hotel we had electricity which was great.

Somebody's Watching Over Me

**Joe Wessels
High school graduation, June 1942**

Our graduating class had 55 students, and I was fortunate to be the salutatorian. After graduating on Thursday evening, I went to work

Monday morning at a tannery for sixty-five cents per hour. I was assigned to the yard gang. The first few days I helped unload cowhides filled with maggots from railroad cars. The stench was almost overwhelming. After that I did a variety of jobs: installing tracks in the railroad yard, working on a roofing gang, in the extract department and a cut-sole department. All the work was hard.

Somebody's Watching Over Me

A section of F Company, Camp Gordon.
Corporal Wessels, front row center

4

Working for Uncle Sam
March 1943 – October 1945

In March 1943, my draft number for the army was picked. I was happy to go. I was sent to Camp Gordon, Georgia, and was made a member of the Third Cavalry Squadron.

This unit began in the Mexican War of 1846–48, commanded by General Winfield Scott. It was Scott who addressed its veterans as Brave Rifles, "baptized in blood and fire [to] come out steel." The Third Cavalry subdued Pancho Villa on the

Mexican border in 1916 and, after World War I, its regimental commanders were Colonels George S. Patton, Jr., and Jonathon M. Wainwright. Rather than prancing horses in World War II, mechanized vehicles made up the cavalry that served as part of Gen. Patton's Third Army in Europe.

Each platoon in the unit does a different job. I was assigned to "F" Company which consisted of light tanks, four officers and 88 enlisted men, and became a tank commander. I was assigned to a tank company and became a tank commander. We had 15 months of very rigorous training.

The two most difficult months of our training were from Nov. 15, 1943, to Jan. 15, 1944, where we participated on maneuvers in the Cumberland Mountains in Tennessee. This was simulated combat. Each man was issued two blankets and half of a tent, called a shelter half. From Sunday at midnight until Friday at midnight, we were constantly on the move and involved with mock combat situations.

When we bivouacked at night, each man took a turn standing on guard duty. We didn't get much sleep. The weather was nasty at times: rain, sleet, snow, and the ground was muddy. We slept on the ground. Our shelter half and two blankets didn't provide much comfort against the elements. Our clothes were summer fatigues which are lightweight garments. We were constantly cold, but were getting trained for combat in Europe.

Normally, military training involves some risk. Prior to going on maneuvers, in one training exercise, our platoon of five tanks lined up side-by-side with about 20 feet between each other, assigned to attack an alleged enemy position a couple hundred yards ahead. I was checking the tanks on either side of me to make sure I was lined up properly. and then turned to look ahead of me. A tree limb was directly in front of my forehead. I dropped in the turret and the limb deflected off my forehead. I was indeed fortunate; otherwise, I might have been decapitated.

In another situation on maneuvers, we were doing a similar training exercise on a plateau atop a mountain. The ground ahead appeared level and had high grass. I was on the far left of our five tanks. Suddenly, my tank lurched to the left and started to slide toward the top of a deep crevasse. My tank became wedged against a large boulder which probably saved our lives. The left track came off, and we were stranded there for three days while our maintenance crew pulled the tank to flat ground and reinstalled the track. We didn't receive any food for the time we were having the tank repaired, so a couple of us went to a nearby farm and stole some chickens. We had a feast.

During my eight weeks of basic training, I had an interesting experience in the first week. My bunkmate was a guy from Bay City, Michigan, whose name was Michael Cricken. At reveille, which I recall was either five o'clock or 5:30 a.m., Mike would stay in his bunk. I told Mike he would get into trouble if he didn't show up for roll call at reveille. He said he wasn't worried because he was being transferred to the paratroops. I asked why he was going to the paratroops. He said, "Because they get $100 per month," while we were getting $50 per month.

So, I immediately requested to be transferred the paratroops. The first sergeant called me into his office and asked me why I didn't like the cavalry and why I wanted to transfer to the paratroops. I told him I liked the cavalry, but I'd get $100 per month in the paratroops. He denied my request and told me to report to the kitchen for KP duty where I stayed for a couple days. It was the only time I was assigned to KP.

So for some reason, the first sergeant -- I didn't like him at the time but he was one of my godsends because he protected me from really hazardous duty. And all through the war, as I reflect back, there were countless times that I should have been killed or seriously wounded and for some reason I was spared.

In high school I played trumpet, so the first sergeant made me the company bugler. Master Sergeant Swift taught James O'Kelly and me all the bugle calls, but O'Kelly backed out to leave me as the only trained bugler While I had to get up before the other men, I didn't have to stand guard duty or work on KP. Also, during basic training, there was a boxing tournament which I entered and boxed as a middleweight. I weighed about 155 pounds and won my weight class.

Middleweight champ

Another thing that happened, we all had to take an IQ test. I scored quite high and the first sergeant took a liking to me. Because in high school I took a year of typing, after maneuvers, the sergeant transferred me from a line platoon to headquarters platoon. I was promoted from a corporal to a technician fourth grade, which is equivalent to a buck sergeant in pay. My job was to serve as liaison between headquarters platoon and the line platoons, similar to a company clerk.

It was a cushy job—no guard duty or KP. I had responsibility for the duty roster which involved assigning men to guard duty and KP duty. I also did other administrative functions.

Meanwhile, I continued with the same training as the other men, learning about the artillery on our tank and other weapons. I was awarded a medal for being a sharpshooter with a carbine. I was also an excellent shot with our other weapons. After basic training, we were given ten days furlough, which was in May 1943. After maneuvers, we were given a 15-day furlough in February 1944.

By June 1944, our training was completed. We boarded a train and went to Camp Schanks, New York, where we stayed for ten days. Every night my buddy, W.W. Stanley, and I would take a train to New York City to see the sights.

One night W.W. and I were having a beer in a bar there and were talking with some merchant marines. They asked if we were going to be shipped out soon. We told them, "Yes," but we didn't know the date. They advised us to sleep on deck if our bunks were on a deck below the waterline because if the ship should be hit by a torpedo, all the hatches below the waterline would be closed in order to keep the ship afloat as long as possible and we would drown. So, W.W. and I slept on deck for the next 15 days while we were going to Liverpool, England.

Somebody's Watching Over Me

**Tech 4 Sgt. Wessels center, Kansas Fleming right,
July 1, 1944**

5

Crossing the Big Pond

Two Army buddies visited me a few months ago and brought me the picture on the facing page. They had found it while in Washington, D.C. at the Army archives. On July 1, 1944, we boarded an English ship, His Majesty's ship, *Synthia*. There must have been at least 100 ships in our flotilla.

After landing in Liverpool, we took a train to London where we witnessed the first sights of war. The German bombers had bombed the railroad yards, and the train tracks were twisted and sticking up in the air like pretzels. The buildings alongside the tracks were burned out. Poor English children ran alongside the train, begging for candy.

Our train left London for a town called Salisbury where the armored equipment was located. We spent the next couple weeks getting our tank in order and zeroing in our artillery. In early August, our squadron moved to Southampton to get on a LST (landing ship, transport) that took us to Cherbourg Beach. While we were in convoy, which was miles long and just inching along, and before getting on the LST, I noticed a building about 50 yards from the road so I ran over to take a look.

Just my luck, it was an English warehouse and nobody was on guard duty. I took a case of tomato juice and grapefruit juice back to my tank. Our captain was standing right beside me, and my sergeant never said a word. Then I returned to the warehouse and took six English wool blankets, and added them to my bedroll of the two blankets that had been issued to me. I believe I had the biggest bedroll in the company. By the end of the war, it was filled with bullet and shrapnel holes, but it did provide some protection against the cold and rainy elements.

While we were crossing the English Channel, each of us was given a sheet that had a few German expressions with English translations. For example:

Nich Schiessen, Don't Shoot
Hända Hoch, Hands Up
Alle Waffen Hinlegen, Lay Your Weapons Down

After disembarking at Cherbourg, we saw the horrors of D-day and the battle of St. Lou.

German tanks that had been destroyed by our bombers were laying in all sorts of positions. Dead bodies were everywhere.

This was the first part of August 1944. We advanced to a town, Avranches, southwest of Paris where we first encountered the enemy behind concealed German machine guns on August 11th. As I dropped into a ditch and bent down in the mud, a mortar slammed into the ridge I had seconds before stood in front of. Luck? Instead of exploding into smithereens upon contact with the ridge, the mortar tilted at an angle and skipped along the surface of the field. Why was I spared, twice?

For the next 273 days, our outfit was on the front line serving as part of the point of General Patton's Third Army. During this time, we had the luxury of one shower in cold water. Our food consisted of C-rations (canned food) or K-rations

Mechanized company entering Sens, Patton's campaign in Northern France, August 21, 1944.

(box). Rarely did we have a cooked meal. Most of the time, we slept on the ground. At times we endured weeks of rain, snow and freezing weather. It was quite an ordeal. War is not glamorous. War is ugly! In my opinion, our country should never wage war based on assumptions.

We participated in four major campaigns for which we received battle stars: Northern France;

Rhineland; Ardennes (commonly known as the Battle of the Bulge); and Central Europe.

Luxembourg, 1945

By May 6, 1945, we had advanced through France, Luxembourg, Germany and Austria to a small picturesque village called Ebensee. I often think of it as a heaven and hell location. We liberated a concentration camp that had about 18,000 starving inmates, who were dying at the rate of 400 per day. I happened to be one of the first soldiers to survey the entire camp with two inmates who guided us through the camp. It was a gruesome sight and an unforgettable experience.

~

The following is a reprinted letter written by Joe for publication by Watson W. Stanley, his buddy from basic training. It appears here all capped as published in the 3rd Cavalry Brave Rifles Bugle, August 1999. *It describes in detail what Joe saw and came upon in helping to liberate this camp, the code name for which was "Zement," part of the Mauthausen network. One also now understands why, years later, Joe does not wish to talk about this experience.*

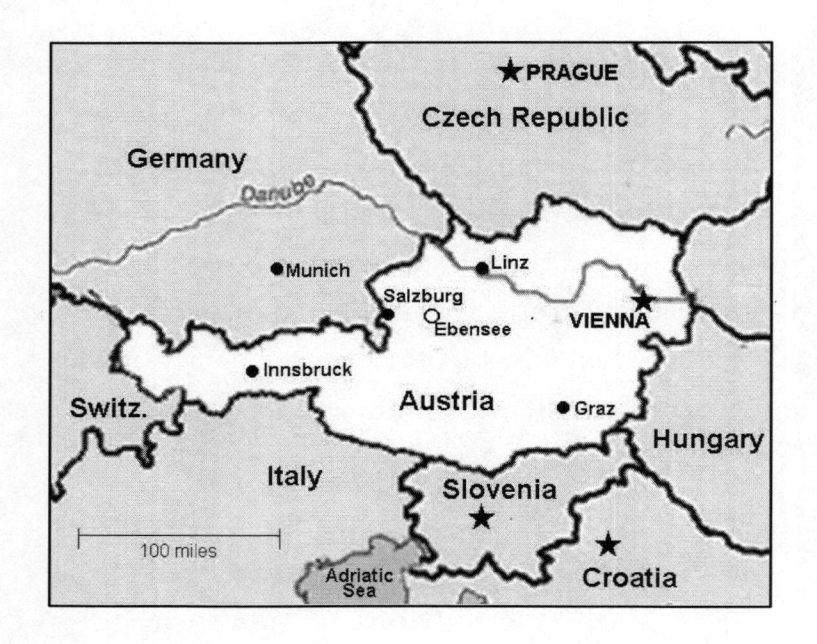

EBENSEE

THE DAY AFTER YOU WERE SERIOUSLY WOUNDED. [MAY 6TH, 1945] WE ADVANCED ALONG A NARROW MOUNTAIN ROAD THAT BORDERED ON LAKE GUMUNDEN GOING TO EBENSEE. THE ROAD WAS WIDE ENOUGH FOR OUR TANKS, BUT CERTAINLY COULD NOT HANDLE TWO-WAY TRAFFIC. IT WAS A

Crossing the Big Pond

BEAUTIFUL DRIVE ALONG THE LAKE WITH THE DEEP BLUE WATER. ON THE OTHER SIDE OF THE LAKE, THERE WERE GREEN MEADOWS AND MOUNTAINS WITH SNOW ON THE PEAKS. WE DID NOT MEET ANY RESISTANCE GOING INTO EBENSEE.

OUR COMPANY "F" 3RD SQUADRON TOOK OVER THE POST HOTEL, WHICH I UNDERSTAND IS STILL THERE. A FEW OF US WERE SETTING UP HEADQUARTERS IN THE HOTEL AND GETTING THE PLATOONS BILLETED IN THE ROOMS. CAPTAIN BRENNAN, SGT. WAKEFIELD AND I WERE TOGETHER GETTING THINGS ORGANIZED. SUDDENLY. TWO EMACIATED MEN WITH SHAVED HEADS AND DRESSED IN FILTHY PRISON UNIFORMS CAME INTO THE OFFICE. THEY TOLD THE CAPTAIN THAT THEY WERE INMATES FROM A CONCENTRATION CAMP LOCATED ON THE OUTSKIRTS OF TOWN. AT THAT TIME, ED MAZUR WALKED IN AND CAPTAIN

BRENNAN TOLD MAZUR AND ME TO GO CHECK IT OUT.

MEANWHILE, DICK POMANTE AND BOB PERSINGER HAD EVIDENTLY BEEN RECONNOITERING ON THE OTHER SIDE OF THE RIVER THAT SEPARATED THE TOWN OF EBENSEE FROM THE CONCENTRATION CAMP. OF COURSE THEY DISCOVERED THE CAMP. AT THE TIME, MAZUR AND I LEFT THE HOTEL WITH THE TWO MEN FROM THE CONCENTRATION CAMP, WE HAD NOT RECEIVED ANY RADIO MESSAGES INDICATING WHAT DICK AND BOB HAD FOUND. AS A MATTER OF FACT, I DIDN'T KNOW UNTIL EITHER 1987 OR 1988 REUNIONS THAT THEY WERE AT THE CAMP BEFORE MAZUR AND ME.

AS I SAID EARLIER WHEN WE ENTERED EBENSEE, WE DID NOT ENCOUNTER ONE GERMAN SOLDIER. I UNDERSTOOD LATER FROM THE CONCENTRATION CAMP INMATES THAT THE SS SOLDIERS FLED THE

CAMP WHEN THEY HEARD AMERICAN SOLDIERS WERE COMING.

MAZUR AND I ARRIVED AT THE CAMP WITH THE TWO INMATES. WE DROVE THROUGH THE GATE AND WERE IMMEDIATELY SURROUNDED BY A MASS OF FILTHY, STARVING MEN. THE TWO INMATES ESCORTED US THROUGH THE ENTIRE CAMP. THEY TOOK US TO THE SO- CALLED INFIRMARY. IT WAS A DEPLORABLE SIGHT--A LARGE NUMBER OF SICK, DYING MEN LAYING IN THEIR OWN FILTH, SOMETIMES WITH 3 AND 4 MEN TO A BUNK SIZED BED WHICH HAD NO MATTRESSES. THE TWO INMATES THEN TOOK US TO THE CREMATORY AREA. ON THE WAY WE SAW STACKS OF CORPSES AND MANY OTHER INDIVIDUAL BODIES.

THE CREMATORY AREA WAS ENCLOSED BY A CHICKEN WIRE FENCE ABOUT 8 FEET HIGH. THERE WAS ONE DOOR GOING INTO THE ENCLOSURE. AT

THE TIME A MAN ENTERED THE CREMATORY AREA, THE GERMAN GUARD WOULD MAKE HIM REMOVE HIS PANTS AND SHOES AND ALLOW THE INMATE TO KEEP HIS SHIRT. INMATES ENTERED THE CREMATORY OF THEIR OWN VOLITION ONCE THEY GAVE UP HOPE OR WERE TAKEN THERE IF THEY COULD NO LONGER WORK. IT WAS THE MOST HORRIFIC SIGHT THAT I EVER SAW. THERE WERE HUNDREDS OF MEN WAITING TO DIE IN FRONT OF US AND THERE WERE *PILES* OF CORPSES.

THE BARRACKS WHERE THE INMATES STAYED HAD DOOR OPENINGS WITH NO DOORS, WINDOW OPENINGS WITH NO WINDOWS AND BARE WOODEN BUNK BEDS WITH NO BLANKETS OR MATTRESSES WHATSOEVER. AND OF COURSE ONCE A MAN ENTERED THE CREMATORY AREA THEY RECEIVED NO FOOD. THE CREMATORY BUILDING WAS A SINGLE STORY BUILDING WITH NO WINDOWS AND IT HAD TWO OVENS. IT WAS

Crossing the Big Pond

POORLY LIT AND AFTER ENTERING THE BUILDING, MAZUR AND I BOTH SAW THE GROTESQUE *BODIES* PILED AGAINST THE SIDE OF THE WALL WITH LEGS AND ARMS STICKING OUT. THE STENCH WAS OVERWHELMING. I THINK I LOST MY SENSE OF SMELL AT THE TIME. BOTH MAZUR AND I WERE SO SHAKEN THAT WE CRIED AT WITNESSING SUCH ATROCITIES.

WHEN WE FIRST ENTERED THE CREMATORY AREA, OUR ESCORTS TOLD THE OTHER INMATES THAT WE WERE AMERICANS. SOME OF THEM CRIED. OTHERS SMILED FEEBLY. THOSE THAT HAD THE STRENGTH TO STAND ASKED FOR A CIGARETTE. I QUICKLY GAVE AWAY THE THREE FROM MY K RATION.

MAZUR AND I LEFT THE TWO INMATES AT THE CAMP WITHOUT ASKING THEIR NAMES. WE REPORTED TO THE CAPTAIN. HE DID NOT MENTION THAT HE HAD ALREADY HEARD FROM DICK AND BOB. WITHIN THE NEXT HOUR HE TOLD BILLY BUCK AND ME T O TAKE

TWO 3/4 TON TRUCKS TO A GERMAN WAREHOUSE THAT WAS DISCOVERED OUTSIDE OF VIENNA. IT WAS DUSK WHEN WE LEFT EBENSEE AND WE RETURNED ABOUT MIDNIGHT LOADED WITH CANNED FOOD. I BELIEVE THE OTHER GUYS WERE ALSO SENT ON FOOD MISSIONS.

MEANWHILE, I AM SURE CAPTAIN BRENNAN HAD INFORMED SQUADRON HEADQUARTERS ABOUT THE CAMP. ALL THE OUTFITS IN THE AREA SENT THEIR COOKS. A MEDICAL OUTFIT ALSO MOVED IN WITHIN TWO DAYS.

IN THE CENTER OF CAMP WAS A HUGE PARADE GROUND. PERHAPS ONE TO TWO BLOCKS SQUARE. ALONG ONE SIDE WERE SEVERAL MESS HALLS. THE COOKS MUST HAVE WORKED ALL NIGHT BECAUSE WE STARTED TO FEED THIS MASS OF STARVING MEN [I'VE HEARD FROM 16,000 TO 18,000] SOMETIME THE NEXT DAY. ALL THE MEN IN OUR COMPANY AND

OTHER COMPANIES WERE ARMED WITH RIFLES. WE FORMED A CORDON AROUND THE FOOD LINE. WE INTERLOCKED OUR ARMS AND WERE TOLD TO ALLOW THE WEAKEST TO GO

FIRST. STARVING MEN ARE ONLY INTERESTED IN SURVIVING AND THE STRONGER WOULD TRY TO PUSH ASIDE WEAKER MEN. SOMETIMES. WE HAD TO BE TOUGH AND PUSH THE STRONGER MEN BACK AND THEN PULL THE WEAKER ONES THROUGH THE CORDON.

WHILE I WAS WAITING IN THE CIRCLE WITH OUR SOLDIERS AND BEFORE WE STARTED FEEDING THE INMATES, I NOTICED A MAN WHO HAD COME TO THE CREMATORY WALK TOWARD ONE OF THE MESS HALLS. HE EXCRETED IN HIS HAND, ATE IT AND DROPPED DEAD. POOR SOUL HAD OBVIOUSLY LOST HIS MIND.

Somebody's Watching Over Me

WHEN I WAS GOING TO WAYNE STATE UNIVERSITY TO GET MY DEGREE AT NIGHT SCHOOL, I TOOK A REQUIRED SPEECH CLASS. ONE NIGHT I GAVE A TALK CALLED "HEAVEN AND HELL, A STONES THROW". IT WAS ABOUT MY IMPRESSIONS OF EBENSEE. THE TOWN WAS AND IS A BEAUTIFUL RESORT AREA—THE SCENERY MAGNIFICENT, BUT THE CONCENTRATION CAMP A GHASTLY NIGHTMARE.

Ebensee mit Traunstein

MAN'S INHUMANITY TO MAN IS BEYOND COMPREHENSION. YET. LOOK AT WHAT HAS

Crossing the Big Pond

RECENTLY HAPPENED IN BOSNIA AND KOSOVO. LET US PRAY THAT GOD WILL EVENTUALLY UPLIFT THE CONSCIOUSNESS OF ALL MANKIND AND APPLY THE GOLDEN RULE "DO UNTO OTHERS AS YOU WOULD HAVE THEM DO UNTO YOU."

WATSON, THIS IS A THUMBNAIL RECAPITULATION OF MY EXPERIENCES, HOPE SOME OF IT WILL BE HELPFUL TO YOU WITH THE BUGLE. IF YOU SHOULD DECIDE TO USE ANY OF IT I'D PREFER TO REMAIN ANONYMOUS. *[HE LATER RECANTED AND SAID I COULD USE HIS NAME.]*

PS. ANOTHER COMMENT. CAN YOU IMAGINE THOSE POOR INMATES WAITING TO DIE IN THE CREMATORY AREA? WE WERE THERE IN EARLY MAY AND EBENSEE IS A MOUNTAINOUS AREA. THE DAYS AND NIGHTS ARE COLD, ESPECIALLY DURING THE WINTER MONTHS. THE INMATES EITHER FROZE OR STARVED TO DEATH.

I HEARD AT THE TIME WE LIBERATED THE CAMP ABOUT 400 INMATES WERE DYING EVERY DAY.

THIS SAD EXPERIENCE LEFT A SCAR ON MY HEART FOR FIFTY YEARS. I RARELY EVER DISCUSSED IT WITH ANYONE AND WHEN I DID, I'D END UP CRYING. SO, NEEDLESS TO SAY I DIDN'T TALK ABOUT IT. NOW. I CAN, BECAUSE I'VE GAINED A DIFFERENT PERSPECTIVE. I'LL TELL YOU ABOUT IT SOMETIME.

~

In May 1945, the Third Cavalry celebrated its 99th anniversary. We assembled in a town called Steyr, Austria, where General Patton was introduced as a great man and addressed our group with language once unfit for mixed company, filled with profanity. He commended us for our efforts in winning the war by first invoking our childhoods:

When you were kids you all admired the toughest boxers. Americans love a winner, and will not tolerate a loser. Americans despise cowards. Americans play to win all the time...You are not all going to die. Only two percent of you here, in a major battle would die. Death must not be feared. Every man is frightened at first in battle...The real hero is the man who fights even though he is scared...The real man never lets the fear of death overpower his honor, his sense of duty of his country and to his innate manhood.

At the conclusion of his speech, he said he hoped to see us on the shores of Japan, "kicking the shit out of those God-damn Japs." An audible sigh swept through the ranks.

We were supposedly experienced combat troops. We boarded a troop train in Austria to be transported to LeHarve, France. It took us ten days to make the trip. The train tracks had been blown up during the war. On our way the train would stop for a few hours, while the track was being repaired. Finally, we arrived at Camp Lucky Strike in LeHarve where we stayed for a few days.

Watson Stanley and Joe

Crossing the Big Pond

Somebody's Watching Over Me

October 1945

6

Post-War Jobs at Home
Detroit, Michigan

On July 1, 1945, we boarded a U.S. Liberty ship and returned to New York City ten days later. It was a thrill to pass the Statue of Liberty. Then we boarded a train that took us to Camp Grant, Illinois. Each of us received a 30-day furlough.

I went to Detroit to see my parents and my sister, Joy. During the last few days of my leave, the United States dropped nuclear bombs on

Hiroshima and Nagasaki. Japan surrendered a few days later. Thank God! Our outfit had been scheduled to go to Fort Bragg, North Carolina, for two month's intensive training to participate in the invasion of Japan. After my leave, I reported to Fort Bragg where I received by discharge from the army near the end of October 1945.

After my discharge, I returned to Detroit. My first job was driving a cab for Checker Cab. While I was driving this cab in Detroit, two incidents occurred within about a month.

One night I picked up a guy who had been drinking, so he kept telling me to go from one place to another. I took him. Finally he said, "My money is up in my apartment and I have to go get it."

So I pulled up in front of the building and I watched the front door and the back door of the building. He didn't go out the back door and didn't come out the front door. After a while I went in and knocked on it, and he didn't answer so I opened the door and went in. There were bottles all over the place. Finally I found him hiding in a closet. I just had been discharged from the Army the week before, so I still had that strong idea of a military concept. I found the guy and dragged him out of there, dragged him down the flight of stairs, threw him in the back of the cab and took him to the police station. The police said, "How did you get him?"

I said, "Well, he didn't come to the door. He owed me $3 and some cents" (talk about stupidity).

"And how did you get him?"

I said, "I opened the door, went in got him up and dragged him out."

The cop said "Did he let you in?"

He called me aside by this time, the police officer, and said "You're trespassing, you broke and entered into his apartment. He could have killed you and gotten off scot-free. You could be locked up."

He turned to the guy and said, "What do you have as collateral to give this cabbie for the three bucks?" He had some meaningful thing.

Two days later the cops called and asked if I wanted a job with the police force. I had just gotten out of the Army and I was not interested in joining up.

About two weeks later, I picked up a pair down in where the patrons start calling you "Whitey" after it gets dark, and you know it's time to get out of there.

Post-War Jobs at Home

I picked up this guy and he kept directing me one place to another. Finally he was leading me off again into some strange place, running up the tab on my meter. And I'm getting farther and farther off the beaten path so I said, "Where are you going?"

He said, "Just keep going, keep going, keep going."

We were going down a dead-end street and, without any warning, a car pulled up behind me and it was a police car. The lights flashed on and they jerked that guy out of the back of the cab, frisked him by the cab and then threw him back in the police car and told me, "Get your butt out of here, just get out of here."

So I could have been killed—but I was protected again. Just seemed like my whole life has been incident after incident where things have come about, through not my doing, but other's doing.

    Meanwhile, I applied for a job with the unemployment agency. Eventually, I got a job the week before Christmas in the shipping and receiving department of a company called Brooks & Perkins, where I was paid $1.15 per hour. They were a fabricator of magnesium products sold to the commercial market, e.g. magnesium griddles. They were good for transmitting heat. The plant employed about 75 people. At the end of January 1946, I was promoted to the purchasing department and became a buyer.

    A few years after I was hired at B&P, the company hired a new executive vice president. Clif Sponsel had contacts with prime contractors who sold military equipment to the U.S. government. Clif did a fantastic job in securing subcontracts and our plant grew to over 1,000 employees within a few years. Fortunately, I received promotions and pay raises. While I was with B&P, the largest contract we received was to build 1,000 tail structures for the B-47 bomber, and I was responsible for all procurement.

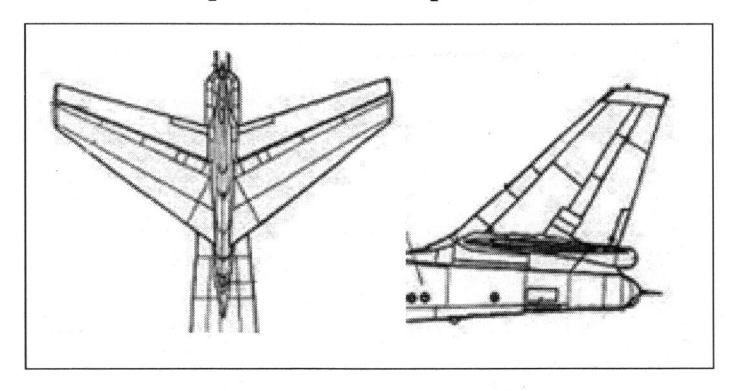

I resigned from Brooks & Perkins on December 31, 1955, after spending ten years with the company. Mr. Perkins took me to the millionaire's club for lunch before I left, which was a special tribute. During lunch Mr. Perkins asked why I was leaving the company and I answered with only one word, "Money." Also, the

Somebody's Watching Over Me

Vice President of Sales, Charlie Vogel, had a farewell party at his home for me.

Post-War Jobs at Home

Somebody's Watching Over Me

Dorothy Street, 1947

7

Dorothy and Me

I mentioned earlier that I graduated from high school in Boyne City. One of my best buddies is a man by the name of Jim Sayles. We are the same age, graduated together and were neighbor kids and I studied at his dad's house to learn how to pass algebra and geometry. Once he got me from a C to an A, I never went back.

Anyway, Jim played all four high school sports—football, basketball, baseball, track—and had a punctured eardrum from football, so he was disqualified from the war. And so he was not serviceable. He went to Detroit, got himself a job at Packard Motor Car Company, went back up to Boyne City and brought his dad down, got him a job at Packard, then went back up again for my dad, and got his a job, also at Packard. My dad had had a heart attack a couple of years before that and never worked afterward. He was always ailing, but learned to use a slip stick (slide rule) on a desk job at Packard.

It was the worst thing I ever did, but it was the best thing: I dated a younger girl. I was working in Detroit at this time; I had elevated from a cab driver to working in a shipping and receiving department in B&P.

One night I stopped at this drugstore where a young clerk was working and asked for a milkshake. She must have liked me because she gave me an extra dip. She was beautiful. She

Dorothy and Me

looked at me, and I'm a hick from the sticks. I was a neophyte. I didn't date when I was in high school. We didn't have boyfriends and girlfriends, at least not where I was from. Maybe a few guys did, but not us—Jim and I didn't—and his brother didn't either.

Dorothy looked like she was 17 or 18 years old to me. I was 21. So I thought to myself a week or so later, I'll take her to a show. So I took her to a show.

Afterwards I asked her, "How old are you?"

She said, "15."

I said, "15?"

Well, I'm kind of stupid, but I knew there were certain laws about that. I didn't see her again for over a year as far as taking her out. I might have gone to get a milkshake, but I never went out with her.

Then when she was 17, I decided, well—now I'll take her out. I found out she was 17. I had been going to St. Paul's Episcopal Cathedral with her and met her parents. I had been working as a cab driver, saving money to buy an engagement ring for Dorothy. I gave her an engagement ring on December 24, 1947, in St. Paul's Cathedral. She turned out to be the best partner I could

Easter, in front of Joe's parent's house, 1949

have ever had. This was in Detroit, at Fourth and Forest.

On May 21, 1948, Dorothy and I were married. We lived in an apartment in a two-story house that her parents had rented out.

It was the greatest blessing of my life. We were blessed with three wonderful children: Janet (April 11, 1952), Joe (December 16, 1954), and Steve (April 17, 1958). We also have six wonderful grandchildren. God has blessed us with a long marriage.

During my tenure with B&P, I attended night school at the Detroit School of Methods Engineering where I learned blueprint reading, estimating and time study. It was basic information but it helped me immensely in my job. I graduated in 1955 with a B.A. in business management from Wayne State University.

Getting my education was a challenging experience that required attending classes three and four nights a week, returning to our apartment where I studied until one or two a.m., arising at six a.m. and going to work from eight a.m. to five p.m. For five straight years I did this, including the summer.

During this time, Dorothy was extremely patient. She never once complained. Our biggest social event was going to a show for fifty cents, or attending church.

A couple months after I graduated from Wayne State, I received an unsolicited phone call from Ford Motor Company, Ford Division, the sales promotion and training department, to invite me for an interview for a position as a statistician. I was accepted for the job and started January 2, 1956.

Dorothy and Me

Somebody's Watching Over Me

In 1958 my boss at Ford said, "Your job comes first, marriage second."

8

My Years at Ford Motor Company 1956 – 1959

My job as a statistician at Ford required me to analyze the major districts outsold by Chevrolet in the United States. Ford's marketing structure was divided into seven regions under which were 35 districts. After ascertaining the worst performing districts, I reported to my manager in the sales promotion and training department. He would assign people to develop programs to assist the districts in increasing sales of Ford vehicles versus Chevrolet.

Somebody's Watching Over Me

A few months after I started at Ford, a new vice president of sales was hired. He made some major changes in our department, and I was assigned to be the editor of a publication called *Ford Crest News*. This paper had a circulation of over 20,000 copies sent to the sales personnel of our seven regions and 35 districts, Ford dealers and salesmen throughout the United States. The publication was behind schedule, but in about three months I managed to get it on schedule.

I didn't like this job, so I complained to a stool pigeon who was a friend of our department manager and managed to be relieved of my job as editor of the *Ford Crest News*.

Next I did market analyses on pilot programs and was sent to various districts to determine the effectiveness of a program to enhance sales of cars and trucks. This was exciting and rewarding work.

My Years at Ford Motor Company

In August 1956, I was assigned to the truck sales promotion & training department. Mr. William C. Scott, "Bill", was my supervisor. He was given the task of developing a 40-hour training program to teach dealer salesmen how to sell light- and medium-duty trucks, and of course, sell cars. People who did this were called combination salesmen if they sold both cars and trucks.

Bill retained the services of a professional writer from a creative agency. I was again thrust into a situation that was foreign to me because I also was given the task of writing lessons, preparing flip charts and flats for teaching manuals to be used by truck trainers. As I stated earlier, there were seven regions in Ford's U.S. marketing operation. Each region was required to appoint a truck trainer. The training program was called the Truck Sales Workshop, which involved 40 hours of in-class sessions. Ford dealers were required to send salesmen to attend the classes.

The Top Hatters were the top salesmen in the company, and knowing who they were helped me do the job assigned to me. At Ford and many other corporations, you learned to keep your mouth shut about the shortcomings of others and to go around them. To contact all the Top Hatters directly by mail was sort of a dumb (smart) mistake. I should have first used the formal "chain of command": go through General Sales to get to each Regional Sales manager, then through the Region to the Districts, and finally to the Dealer.

Jumping the chain was not appreciated and even though I did it out of ignorance, somehow I was protected by an unseen guardian and eventually offered promotion to an exciting alternative.

My Years at Ford Motor Company

Bill, the creative writer, and I completed the initial development of the Truck Sales Workshop in about three months. Bill held two training sessions with the seven trainers to familiarize them with the program and had them practice using the script, flip charts, flats, etc. I assisted Bill in making sure all the training materials were available.

After the training sessions, the trainers returned to their respective regions to implement the program with the dealer salesmen. I became the national coordinator of the program and was the contact man at Ford division for the trainers. The trainers advised me of the cities where they were going to hold the program, and I would arrange to send the necessary training material for the session to be held.

The trainers were also required to send a report to me of the number of salesmen attending and trucks sold by each salesman before and after the program. I kept records of this data to determine the efficacy of the Truck Sales Workshop. The results were outstanding. I don't recall the specifics, but one of my reports stated the truck sales statistics for the salesmen who attended the workshop. This report eventually went to Mr. Ford who said, "Let's have more of them."

From August 1956 through October 1959, I served as the national coordinator of the Truck Sales Workshop. Mr. Scott quit Ford and started his own business. Then I reported to Frank Zimmerman, Truck Sales Promotion & Training Manager. Frank reported to Lee Iacocca, Truck Marketing Manager.

Fortunately, I was well-liked by the trainers and the people in our department. I was offered a big promotion which would have required full-

My Years at Ford Motor Company

time travel. After discussing this opportunity with my wife Dorothy, I initially accepted. At that time, we had three wonderful children (who all grew up to earn college degrees): Janet was seven; Joe, four; and Steve, one, but I didn't like the idea of being gone all the time from my family. One week after I accepted the new position, Frank Depatie, my brother-in-law, offered me 40 percent of his business, so I resigned my job with Ford and moved our family west to Kalamazoo, Michigan.

Janet, 1956

Joe and Steve, 1960

Depatie Fluid Dynamics

Fluid Connections

WEST MICHIGAN HYDRAULICS

NuCon Systems

DEPATIE FLUID POWER

FORD MOTOR COMPANY

Brooks & Perkins

🏁 Checker Cab 🏁

9

Kalamazoo, Here We Come!
1959 – Present

In September 1959, I notified Zimmerman that I was leaving in two weeks. He asked me to stay with Ford. Actually, I stayed until the end of October. During that time I conducted a three-day meeting with the seven trainers in Chicago to review the training materials in the Truck Sales Workshop to determine if any changes were necessary. The trainers were aware that I was resigning from Ford and gave me a slide film projector as a farewell gift. Zimmerman had a

Halloween party at his home for us with all my associates and their wives. They presented us with an eight place setting of sterling silverware. This was a lavish gift.

The end of October 1959, we moved our family to Kalamazoo, Michigan. I started employment with Depatie Fluid Power the first week of November. There was only Frank and me with a one part-time employee. Both of us served as salesmen. Of course, Frank became president and I became secretary-treasurer, and eventually sales manager.

When we moved to Kalamazoo, we moved into a little house on Clover Street. Shortly after we were getting into business, we organized a company called NuCon Systems, a distributing company to promote the sale of aerologic components for use with electrical devises. I had fun naming it, choosing a phonetic shorthand

Kalamazoo, Here We Come!

spelling for "**p**n**eu**matic **con**trols" and using some marketing savvy from my Wayne State business degree.

Frank said, "I'm the president of Depatie so you be the president of NuCon." We each owned 50 percent of NuCon at this time. We later organized another company called West Michigan Hydraulics which was in the hydraulics field.

Later we organized still another company in Grand Rapids called Fluid Connections, also distributors in the same industry as ours. To eliminate conflicts of interest which might have happened if we had just blossomed into one huge company, we separated different customer bases and set up different management for each smaller company.

I started it really. I had lunch with Jim Chambers who was a salesman for Parker-

Hannifin, and asked him how he would like to go into business.

I said, "Get a piece of paper out." So he got a napkin out.

I said, "How much volume do you think you could do the first year?

He said, "I think I could do this,"

I said, "Write it down."

He said, "You understand I'm going to control this business."

I said, "No, you're not. Frank and I are each going to have 30 percent and we'll give you 40 percent, and we'll give you an option to buy out after so many years."

Since then I don't know what's happened to West Michigan Hydraulics, but I do know now the

Kalamazoo, Here We Come!

companies are flourishing under John Thomas, Carl Moretti and Joe Melwiki. Jim Chambers is still going strong with his company. These companies have been subsequently sold to various other entities and now they are still doing fine.

Our company, Depatie Fluid Dynamics, prospered. We sold our respective interests in 2002 to our eight employees, a great group of guys.

About a week after we first moved into our little house on Clover, Dorothy said "Is this the best you can do?"

I said "It's the best we can do here, but don't worry we'll be in clover some day."

Somehow, miraculously, Dorothy found a house in the Golden Triangle at 1216 Lakeway. It was an old Cape Cod that backed up to the Milham Golf Course. It had three bedrooms and two baths upstairs and it was a lovely house.

"If you buy this house I'll never ask for another thing again," she said. We bought it with depreciated Ford stock as a tax write-off.

Kalamazoo, Here We Come!

We were there about two years. I got tired of taking down the storms in the springtime and putting up screens and washing the windows while all my buddies were out playing golf, so I sold the house—in one day. One Saturday I put a For Sale sign in the yard, and a neighbor's minister bought it on sight.

We made money on the house and moved into an apartment over at Milwood Apartments, which also backed up the golf course and became a staging area for friends waiting to build their own houses. It had a swimming pool in the complex for the kids in the summertime and was conveniently located for me.

In our building a neighboring couple, who had lost their firstborn, had recently brought home a newborn baby. The mom became audibly hysterical one afternoon when her baby wasn't responding at naptime, and our ten-year old son

Joey somehow had the presence of mind to dial 911. Help came within minutes to save that neighbor's baby.

We stayed there until about 1966 when we bought a lot over on Holiday Lane. We designed and built a colonial house on Holiday Lane in 1965. Miller-Davis Company constructed it with a big kitchen and huge family room with piped music and a bar to entertain friends. We were lucky because the price of real estate was going up so we stayed on Holiday Lane, I think, until

1425 Holiday Lane

Kalamazoo, Here We Come!

about 1980 or '81.

Dorothy was always sweeping up the patio probably due to her Dutch upbringing. One day I came home from work and asked if she had fertilized the lawn. I hadn't noticed that she had arranged to remove a huge oak tree during the day, telling the workers they had to get it all done between 8 AM and 5 PM. Just as I had had enough of putting up and taking down screens on our Lakeview house, she had had enough of sweeping up leaves

We sold the house on Holiday Lane and moved to a bigger house on Hidden Cove. We sold that house in 2005 and moved here to Stonehedge.

My life has been filled with joy, happiness, health, and abundance. God has blessed me.

My Friendship with Aziz Hamdy

Dorothy and I developed a good friendship in about 1970 or thereabouts with a couple who lived in our neighborhood, Aziz and Heide Hamdy. They were both from Egypt. Aziz was a senior scientist at Upjohn and a devout Muslim. He made three trips to Mecca, but he was not a fanatical person at all. He was just a kind, loving person.

Dorothy and I went to Egypt with them in 1975 for some particular business venture that didn't pan out. A few years later, about 1980 or thereabouts, Aziz started complaining of blood in his stool. He ended up having colon cancer.

Dr. Peake, another friend of ours, came up and said, "Aziz just bought a ticket out of here, he's gone. He has colon cancer and it's going to migrate into the liver or some other part of his body."

Kalamazoo, Here We Come!

The night that this news came, Dorothy was there with Aziz's wife, Heidi. Aziz asked the girls to leave the room. When Aziz was alone with me, he said. "Would you do me a favor?"

I said, "I'll try to do what you want."

He said, "I want you to conduct my funeral."

I said, "Wait a second, Aziz. I try to be a Christian, but I'm not a Muslim."

He said, "Do you believe in God?"

I said, "Yes, I believe in God."

He said, "Well, you are my brother and I want you to do my funeral."

I thought about it for a few seconds and then said, "Okay, I'll do it."

We lived down the block from Aziz and Heidi when we were on Holiday Lane. So I read the Qu'ran for several months in preparation to do this. Every night I went up to see Aziz and we discussed what I had read in the Qu'ran. I don't remember unfortunately too much now, but it made a lot of sense at the time:

> *And the Prophet was considered illiterate, he could neither read nor write. And he would often go off by himself into the countryside and pray and meditate, and the archangel Gabriel appeared to him and said, "You are to tell your people." So he'd start dictating to him what he's supposed to tell the people in Arabic and he said everywhere I looked he would appear. And so he said. I turned my head this way he'd be there; turn my head that way, and*

he is there. So he went back and he found a scribe. From memory he would translate or tell, recite what he had been told by the archangel Gabriel.

At that time the Arabic clans were practicing, I don't know what the word is now, but they were killing their baby girls. They would bury them alive. They kept their baby boys because the boys could become farmers or warriors and they needed them. But the girls were a drag because they required a dowry to get rid of them. You had to give a camel or sheep or goats or whatever you had to get rid of them.

And at that time there was a system as far as diet. People were eating unsanitary things, so they tried to teach the society through the revelations about proper eating. They practiced idol worship, and he tore the idols down just like

Moses did, just like Christ did in the temple. These guys have a lot in common, these spiritual leaders, I think.

As far as now where these terrorists are coming from, but then I don't need to go very far because look what has been happening in Ireland for the last hundred years or more. The Protestants and the Catholics have been killing women and children, and they all believe in Christ.

The official had to prepare the body for burial, and I had the job of washing part of Aziz's body. He was a wonderful person. Aziz always said, "You're like a brother to me." After the funeral some Muslims came to our house and wanted me to turn Muslim. I replied politely, "Thank you, but I try to be a Christian."

Kalamazoo, Here We Come!

Another Trip

Dorothy and I took a trip to China in 1997. The Great Wall of China is one of the wonders of the world. We went to the city of Xian. Near there are hundreds of terra cotta soldiers created by Emperor Qin Shi Huang, the first of ancient Chinese emperors, in the third century B.C. There were horses all carved out, men with armor on them, full-sized people, in a big amphitheater filled with these immense figures. And they looked so authentic.

We saw and met the man who had the good luck to find everything that now attracts tourists when he was a farmer digging a well in 1974. He brought up this piece of pottery and from then on it just exploded. By 1987 UNESCO had named the site part of the world's cultural heritage.

Summer 2007 — The Great Gatsby Event of My Life!

This doctor said, "You go to your friend's 60th and look what happened to you, the 60/60/40 Party, and look what happened to you."

The party was absolutely—I was trying a think of the book, *The Great Gatsby*, he was a gangster, I believe, that had a beautiful party out on the river, the band was playing and it was just gorgeous. But it was—it was just overwhelming.

Our dear friends, Pat and Carl Moretti, whom we have known for 40 years were going to have their combination birthday party and wedding anniversary, called the 60/60/40 Party. And even though I was ailing, I was determined to go to that party to show my respect to those

Kalamazoo, Here We Come!

Carl, Joe and Dorothy at Gun Lake, Summer 2007

wonderful people. Somehow, in spite of Dorothy's harassment and the chains I was trying to break out of, I got out there to Gun Lake.

And lo and behold Carl, whom I have known for 40 years because we worked together for all those years, when he saw me, he was crying and I started to cry. I said "What's this all about?" He was so glad to see us.

And then 15 minutes later his daughter, Missy, comes up. She is a great musician and starts to serenade me with her saxophone right in front of me. And I don't remember the song, but I was so overwhelmed with joy I just couldn't imagine it.

Danielle Sanders in our home

I was crying, Carl was crying kneeling by me, Dorothy was crying, Danielle, the young girl who takes care of me was crying (she is my angel in this physical body here). Then when Missy was leaving, I happened to spot Pat and said, "Do you suppose she could play 'God Bless America' because it's one of my favorite songs too?"

She said, "I don't know, we'll try." Pat approached Missy and the next thing I know they were playing "God Bless America." The whole group of people stood up; some were crying during the rendition of "God Bless America." It was just a beautiful sight.

Everybody was touched. It was a joyous occasion for Pat and Carl, but also it brought such goodness out of everybody in the audience. We were all united.

Somebody's Watching Over Me

Rose Arbor corridor, 2007

10

Volunteering for Hospice

I was involved in our business pretty much on a full time basis until about 1990. Then I started to phase out. I thought, "Wow, now I've got time to play a little more golf, do a little more tennis playing and enjoy the fruits of life." I did that for a couple of months and finally concluded there's got to be more things that are meaningful than just pleasure.

At that time I initially, then Dorothy and I, got involved in our Episcopal church, St. Luke's, visiting patients in hospitals. But whenever we went there, nobody was there from our parish. I thought there's got to be somebody else.

It was then that I learned about Hospice. The initial organization for the office was in St. Luke's office building. Because Father Holt authorized it, I called in and said, "I'd like to become a Hospice volunteer."

"Well, that's great," he said. I had to go through training, which I did. I forget the number of days I was in training, but it was very interesting. That was 1991.

In Hospice I found out that there were other things than just being competitive all your life. In life you are working in a competitive environment, as I was doing in marketing and sales. But in Hospice, your purpose is to be compassionate, kind, considerate, caring and loving for other people who have no expectation of anything in return.

It gave me a great deal of personal satisfaction to know that I was comforting a person who was having some problems, while the fellow's wife had gone to get her hair done or go to lunch and have some time away from the house.

Drawing for the story, "Win by Losing"

Oftentimes I played cards or games with people who liked to do that. Sometimes you found your match and it was really a pleasure. With some people who were terminally ill, I decided it was better to let them win rather than me. I would make mistakes in the game deliberately so they would end up winning the game. Beth Carroll Van Houten interviewed me a few years ago before writing the story, "Win by Losing," later published in the book, *Living Well, Dying Well: Stories from Rose Arbor Hospice,* which told of my driving away with a smile on my face.

Male volunteers are always assigned, or at least when I was calling on them, to male patients who were ill. I would take people for rides in the car, sometimes to hospitals, and would get their medicines.

The first patient assigned to me was David, a husky, young 18-year old, with terminal cancer. Fleshy, not too coordinated. He was like a grandson to me and reminded me of one of my own sons.

One day we tried playing golf at the Kalamazoo Country Club at no charge, but David didn't have much strength swinging his club and he fell down on the course so we couldn't pursue the game. His mom the next day told me he didn't want to go today. Every time I called she was in tears, feeling guilty because her son getting

cancer and having Hepatitis B too.

I suggested to David that we didn't have to play golf, but we could go to KCC anyway, maybe just chip and putt or just have lunch. That was OK. Over lunch I asked David if he ever helped around the house—you know, took the garbage out, vacuumed—or told his mom that you appreciate her?

"No."

"Did you ever write her a letter, telling her how grateful you are?" Another time I asked, "Ever buy your mom flowers?" After an outing one day, David brought home a beautiful bouquet of flowers. His mom was so happy.

And you know what? At his funeral, the minister read his letter to his mom. My heart overflowed that he had so much gratitude that he was able to give.

Another hospice patient assigned to me was a man about 50 years old with brain cancer named John. His way of being in the world when I got to know him was always to keep his head down while repeating a sort of mantra, "I don't know what I'm going to do. I don't know what I'm going to do."

Finally, one day I thought I'd give him an example of what he might do. "Have you ever said 'thank you' to the aide who brings in your meals or to the nurse who rearranges your pillows trying to make you more comfortable?"

I was wearing a red golf shirt that he gently took hold of when I next stopped to visit with him. He wasn't repeating his mantra, and he looked at me all the while rubbing my shirt together between his fingers in a way that felt like our souls were connecting.

One of the first times I went to see a patient, he said, "Joe, you want a little moo-moo juice?"

I said, "What's moo-moo juice?"

He said, "Black Velvet."

I said, "No, thank you. By the way, is this allowed on your program?"

He said, "Yes, I can have two shots a day." So, who was I to question him? Two shots a day?

His wife was especially well-endowed. They were short stocky people from the Upper Peninsula, of Finnish descent. She must have had a 60-inch bosom which caused an abscess under her arm from rubbing on her flesh. The doctor said she should have a breast reduction. One day as I was getting ready to leave my friend (they lived in a lower basement apartment), she said, "Joe, I'd like to talk to you privately."

I went outside with her and she tells me that the doctor recommended a breast reduction and that she'd have to be in the hospital away from her husband, and he would get all concerned. She asked, "What do you think I should do?

I said, "I think you ought to do what the doctor says." Wow, I wanted to know where was the nearest exit when it gets that personal.

I guess I can give nicknames. His nickname was Anch. Anch grew up in the U.P. and one of his buddies' father owned a delicatessen that served anchovies. The owner of the delicatessen was always finding shortages in his anchovies because these kids were helping themselves.

One night the owner caught them down by the railroad tracks eating the anchovies that they had stolen. From then on he got the nickname "Anch," and it stuck with him all his life. He was really a nice man.

Anyway, his wife finally did have the surgery and they moved him from his home to Bronson Care Center down in Vicksburg. I went out there to see him. He said, "Joe, my wife's got a boyfriend; she doesn't call me and she doesn't come to see me."

I said, "How long you been married?"

He said, "Oh, I don't know, almost 60 years."

"Believe me, Anch, she doesn't have a boyfriend, it's something else. I mentioned to you that she went in for surgery so she was in the hospital," and I went home.

I know that Dorothy had not had Hospice training, but nevertheless I said, "Dorothy, I've got a real special case so you come with me."

We stopped and got some flowers to take out to Anch. He immediately brings up that his wife's got a boyfriend. I had Dorothy's female presence say, "You're mistaken, Anch, that's incorrect."

Anyway, they released Anch from the hospital and put him up near Rose Arbor. There is a place up there near Hospice which has extended care. It's right off West Main -- Bronson Place. I went in there to see him. He said "Joe, do you have any moo-moo juice?"

"No, but I have some Canadian Club and Crown Royal."

"Oh," he said, "that would be wonderful." My initial thought was I'll go get a McDonald's milk shake and dump it out and put some stuff in there and take it out to him.

I called the director of volunteers and she said, "Absolutely not." That killed that.

A day or two later Dorothy and I were going to an Army reunion in Las Vegas. Although I'd already seen Anch that day, I thought I'd stop and see him one more time. When I got there, he was all smiles.

"Joe, come on, I want to show you what I've got." His wife had gone out and bought him a half gallon of Black Velvet, and he was giggling.

He said,: "You know, I'm only supposed to take a shot at one time, but she gave me two shots." So he took two shots. and it was the last time I saw him. He had a heart attack that night. Evidently it was too much for his system, but he died with a smile on his face.

When I was selling tickets for Hospice's Duck Race, Joe Melwiki didn't know that I worked in Hospice. He said, "Gee, my grandparents say there is this nicest guy that called on them."

I said, "What's your grandparents' name?" Names are all confidential at Hospice.

He told me "Anch."

I said, "I'm the guy that has been calling on your grandparents."

Rykse's cinnamon buns are enormous.

In addition to calling on people in their homes, I decided to get into bereavement training as a facilitator. I went through some bereavement training courses where they had monthly breakfasts at Rykse's Restaurant. We would have from 12 to 20 people there, all men, who had lost their spouses. It just gave the men an opportunity to sit around and share their words and their losses, memories, and it was quite a comfort, I think, to those people. I did that for several months.

At that time I was retired from my business so we went to Florida. I immediately signed up for Hospice training while I was in Florida where I could play golf and tennis, too. I did the same thing down there, calling on people who were convalescing in homes.

The first patient I had, I said to the lady "When would you want me there?"

She said, "How about one o'clock?"

I said, "Okay I'll be there at one."

So I got there and I remember, I have a good memory about this, his name was Earl. As she was leaving, she said, "When do you want me back?"

I said, "Whenever you want to come back."

She said, "How about next week?" They get punchy after a while, the caregivers. His wife leaves home. My patient is a man by the name of Earl.

He quickly says, "Could you give me a Chesterfield?" (He is dying of lung cancer.) Well, that stunned me. I went to the phone the next day and called the director of volunteers and she said, "If that's what they want, that's what they have. It's their choice. We are not there to heal, just to comfort."

You run into all kinds of patient situations. Being a Hospice volunteer has certainly taught me to be a more compassionate, sympathetic, empathetic kind of person, and to understand the loss that other people experience when they have the loss of a loved one.

I assisted Hospice both in Kalamazoo and Florida, in fundraisers like golf outings. I made phone calls to help them. Actually, when Dorothy and I were in Florida, somebody told me about a Hospice house similar to what is now Rose Arbor. I said, "Gee, we need to have something like that in Kalamazoo."

We were going to come home the next week. Before we came home I called the director down there and he said, "Sure we've got a place down here that has about a hundred patients in it. We have one over here, like a neighborhood."

Something that's like a neighborhood atmosphere, that's what I want. We went to visit it, and it had rooms for about 12 people. I said, "That's just perfect."

There were children in the neighborhood. You could hear the voices, dogs barking, just a neighborhood environment.

When I got home, the first thing I did was go down and see the director here. She said,

"Somebody had just given Hospice $250,000 anonymously. That's what we are going to do, find some land to build Rose Arbor."

And that's where it started. But anyway, when I was walking with a cane or with a walker, I was out there making calls on people at Rose Arbor. I would walk in.

One of the patients at Rose Arbor was about 90 years old, terminally ill with aneurysms. I said to the nurse, "How come he keeps on going, month after month. Why don't they have the surgery?"

"Well, it's kind of risky."

"But how does he keep on going?"

"Well, the body has a natural way of sort of healing these lesions inside by building up plaque over the sore spot so that it doesn't split."

When I got ready to go to Florida, I would go in to see him, I forget, his home. He was in Petoskey and I was from Boyne City, and we had a lot of good visits together. I walked in there in my damn walker and every time I would get ready to get up to leave, he would say, "Let me help you get up."

Here was this old guy 90 years old, ready to die, helping me to get up!

Helper, Teacher, Mentor?
You Never Know Who May Need You

When our son Steve was in high school, he was dating a young girl, Debbie, and going to Portage Northern. They both were good students and went to Michigan State together. Debbie was attracted to another young man up there, a little older man. His name was Derk.

Derk came over to the house—this was 25, 30 years ago now—and we had a beer at the bar in our house and talked. He was in martial arts, and I must have said something to him at that time that affected him.

I got a surprise this year. First of all, we got a call from Michael Depatie and his wife, Holly, who said they had just seen Derk in Maui, Hawaii. Michael said, "There is a tie between you and Derk; he is always asking about you, wondering how is Joe, how is Joe?" He said, "We just got back and saw Derk." Well, 15 minutes later the phone rang and who was on the phone, but Derk.

He said, "How are you doing, Joe? I hear you're not doing too well. I just wanted you to know that you said something to me 30 years ago that changed my life. I've always thought of you and had respect for you, and wish you well."

What it was I said, I have no idea.

We were talking about the veterans of the Vietnam War the other day.

My son-in-law's brother, Dick, who is a Vietnam vet, lives as a recluse in Traverse City. We went out for a Christmas dinner a few years ago, and Dick was there. Dick looked to me like he was 70, long hair, long beard, never married and a very kind man. His father said when he came home, got out of the service, he would wake up screaming and crying. He must have gone through some real turmoil while he was in Vietnam.

Dick put his arm around my neck at the table and said to me, "Joe, you saved my life."

I said, "Why? How?"

He said, "Twenty years ago when I got out of Vietnam, I was a basket case, and you said something that helped save my life. The reason I'm alive today is because of you."

I started to cry and he started to cry. What did I say? I really don't know.

Another fellow, Chip—a nice guy, maybe 46, 47—said, "Joe, you're a teacher. Everywhere you go, you help people get along in their life better."

Danielle, my little helper, says the same thing. So, that's what I think I'm here to do—help people.

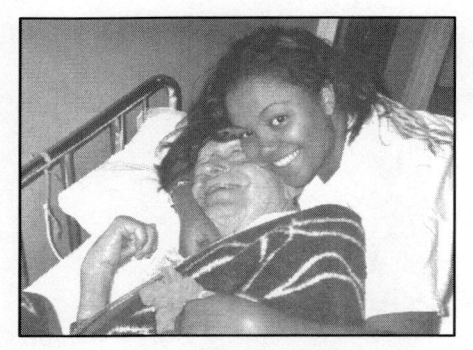

**Joe and Danielle's
nightly routine**

When I think about it, at my birthday party up here this year, it was like my wake. There were so many kind things said that I guess I've had a purpose in living that makes me feel good. I hope I still have a purpose for still being here because it isn't fun anymore. You know when you have to rely on everybody to help you get on the john, get in the shower, out of the shower, get in bed, feed you, it's just that you feel like you've lived as much of this life as you're going to do, just about, or want to. What more can I do?

Volunteering for Hospice

Somebody's Watching Over Me

11

Philosophy of Life

My early life was spent growing up during the 1930s, years of the Great Depression. It was a difficult time for the majority of people. I recall one family of five boys whose parents had died. They lived in a primitive house with broken windows that had been covered with scraps of wood in an attempt to keep out the cold winter months. All the boys served in the military during World War II. Three of them were killed. Many other families lived in similar conditions.

In many respects I was fortunate because both my parents were alive and did what they could to encourage my sister and me. As I mentioned earlier my dad had a heart attack when I was about 13 and was unable to work. My mother got jobs as a cook in a restaurant, resort hotels and the Dilworth Hotel in Boyne City (in 2006, the hotel was still there). During this period, until I joined the army in March 1943, I also worked at a variety of jobs. The money I earned went to my mother. As I reflect back, I learned to be self-reliant, responsible, accountable, confident, respectful and dependable. So, this adverse period turned out to be a life-long blessing.

Our family did not attend church, but somehow I acquired a strong belief in God, even before I met Dorothy's family in Detroit. They attended St. Paul's Episcopal Cathedral where we became engaged in 1947, and she will always be

Philosophy of Life

an Episcopalian. One of the prayers in the little book Aunt Ella gave me when I was a kid was this one:

> *Now I lay me down to sleep,*
> *I pray the Lord my soul to keep.*
> *If I should die before I wake,*
> *I pray the Lord my soul to take.*

During the Depression there were economic/philosophic organizations that evolved that were intended to improve the standard of living of people. My dad became involved in an organization called the Direct Credits Society. One of its principles was to eliminate interest charged for borrowing money. I don't recall how banks were supposed to function or how businesses and individuals would have been able to borrow money.

A man by the name of Alfred Lawson was the founder of the Society who authored several books. When I was about 12 or 13, my dad required me to read these books. I recall the books were titled: *Physical Manifestation, Emotional Manifestation, Mental Manifestation.* Reading these books provided me with concepts that gave me a foundation for my present spiritual beliefs.

Lawson taught there is a Cause and Effect in all creation. In other words, what a person thinks about is most likely to come about. There is only Energy. Each individual has the power to use the Energy either positively or negatively to influence conditions that occur in their own life or the lives of others. As Jesus taught, "As a person sows, so shall you reap."

Another important incident in my life getting involved in the Coptic philosophy in 1985. Subsequent to the Coptic philosophy, I became familiar with a group called the Movement of

Philosophy of Life

Spiritual Inner Awareness (MSIA) which was founded by John-Roger and also John Morton. The purpose of this organization is to teach an initiate to attain total transcendence in this lifetime, to become more familiar that we are a living soul occupying a physical body

To me, God is all Loving. He created the universe and our Soul in His spiritual image. Each soul is an eternal part of God, and that soul evolves through eons of experiences until It merges back with the Godhead. Thus, there are no lost souls and there is no Hell, fire and brimstone because God will not destroy part of Himself.

I have learned three basic principles to guide my life:

> 1. Take care of myself so I can take care of others.

2. Don't hurt myself and don't hurt others.

3. Use every experience to enhance my growth.

As Jesus said, "Love thyself, as you love others."

After reviewing the experiences I've had in my life, I realize that I have been blessed with either angelic energy or the energy of Christ's Holy Spirit to surround and protect me from outside harm and negative influences. This Energy always helps me make the right decisions to what I should do to protect myself, and guide me in the right way.

Having lost in 1969 whatever Episcopal orthodoxy I had picked up, later I drove to Detroit on Tuesday evenings in 1985 to listen to Master John-Roger lecture on the Movement for Spiritual

Inner Awareness. First of all, to become involved in MSIA, one has to write to John-Roger and request to become his initiate or student. If he accepts you, he will respond. Eventually I was accepted as his student.

Then the initiate is requested or required to buy a dozen booklets a year called Discourses and also a dozen spiritual awareness training tapes. And the initiate was allowed to read one booklet at a time, and he or she could read previous booklets as many times as they wish

For $100 a year I bought and read his Discourses which were for personal use only, and I have read 12 years of them. Now tapes are available for $100 a month.

So, since 1985 I have been involved with MSIA and I read all the Discourses every couple of years. After you go through enough inner spiritual experiences, John-Roger will write and say you are ready for your next initiation. You go in front of one of his followers who will give you a mantra that you recite inwardly.

So going through all the initiations now and in 1998, I became ordained as a minister of the silent order. My mission wasn't to preach, it was to go out and do good in life.

"My" philosophy is not actually mine, but that of John-Roger. Basically, it's take care of yourself so you can take care of others.

As I'm approaching the twilight years of my life, I know that my days are getting shorter. It will be a blessing from God when he finally does take me. I can only say thanks to everybody for all the love that they have given me. We have people that come over all the time.

Today I am not afraid to die. Death just means that the physical part of me will rot away, but the soul that my body wraps around will reunite with the soul of the Creator.

"Then why do you keeping taking your pills?" Dorothy has asked me. Any more time I can have to become more Christ-like and use that opportunity to pass on those behaviors to others is reason enough to follow my doctor's advice.

Somebody's Watching Over Me

**Tuna and durado caught off Cabos St. Lucas,
Baja California, Mexico, 1996**

12

Looking Back

Dorothy's older sister, Todd, married Frank DePatie, a business partner. Their three kids— Diane, Kit and Michael— are like our own. We all lived in the same neighborhood and our kids played together, went to the same church and schools. We have always been very close to them, loving them just as much as we do ours, and they love us as a second set of parents. Many times we took them on family trips: up north to Harbor Springs in the summer and to Florida in the winter.

I loved to take family trips, the boys fishing and hunting, even to Bimini, and I took the girls to a dude ranch near Alpena. Once with all the kids and our black dog, Onyx, a bat that was in our cabin connected with a well-aimed swat from my newspaper.

It was important to me that I be a good provider. One of the things I tried to do often was take family vacations. Several times we took trips to Canada to go fishing in the fall for walleye and pike. It was a great experience for everybody. We had shore lunches—don't salivate—but it was so delicious. We would transport groups to camp by seaplane on Cape Anapagome, Ontario.

Looking Back

Flights ahead of us got there safely, but as our plane took off, a dark thunderstorm came up and the pilot decided it was such a threat, he was going to shorten it and land in the middle of a lake. A hell of a jolt! Steve and I were on that flight, which was very precarious. You could see the lights of the cabins around the lake.

Steve is a naturally curious person. He makes friends easily and got to know the families at the lodge where we all received free food and a night's lodging. At daybreak, we took off to join the other fishing camp group.

Steve

Somebody's Watching Over Me

Steve gave me an essay he wrote for a Mr. Andrews' third-hour Behavioral Science class, with this note, "There ya go, Pops. I saved it for ya because I knew ya wanted the paper":

Father

My father, he's one in a million. His activities are strange to me, but mine probably are rather odd to him also. My dad is a salesman, for Depatie Fluid Power. He travels across the state selling valves, hydrolics [sic] and O Rings. He shows much interest and motivation in his job.

Another time-consuming occupation he is involved with is, he's a teacher for a philosophy called Coptic Religion. This philosophy is a good one. It teaches you to have self confidence, self control, proper breathing exercises, exercises, meditation, correct eating habits and other knowledge of the conscious & subconscious mind. Many of the teachers are vegetarians like my father. To have good health and eating habit, his diet consists of vegetables, fish, cheese, milk, or any non-meat food. All the food he eats he buys at the health food store.

The busy schedule he has does not take him away from his family. We go on many trips with our family. Sometimes my dad takes me on fishing, hunting and skiing trips. Just the two of us. He enjoys going on trips together.

Over all, my father is a great example of a good father. He is happy and content always. He tries never to loose his temper and talks all problems out verbally. With his spare time he reads books on Power of the Mind, Self Control of Body & Mind. He tries to read everything pertaining to the Mind or Body. My father enjoys everything he is involved with. He's a happy individual.

When they were kids, Steve was known as the "mouth," while Joe was "brawn." Dorothy and I often cautioned him that his mouth would get him into trouble. While Steve was dating Debbie, they went to a drive-in movie and some motorcycle guys pulled on her blouse at the shoulder. Amazingly, he kept his mouth shut but came home and told his brother Joe. I advised them both to forget about the incident because of likely retaliation, but it turned out that Joe went after the guys and beat them up.

Joe C

Years before that we went to a dude ranch-type resort in Montana. Sometimes kids don't follow every safety instruction adults may give them. Horseback riding activities were not an exception. Little Joe came running to me one day saying that Janet fell off her horse and her head was bleeding. When I ran out I saw her on the

Looking Back

ground with her head wrapped in a blood-soaked towel and I could see the bones in her head. The resort doctor told us to give her a few aspirin and she'd be alright in the morning. I thought she needed immediate hospital care so I took her to the nearest town. The doctors there said she needed more care than they could give and recommended a hospital 100 miles away. I wanted to charter a plane right then but they told me that in Montana there was no speed limit and we could drive there just

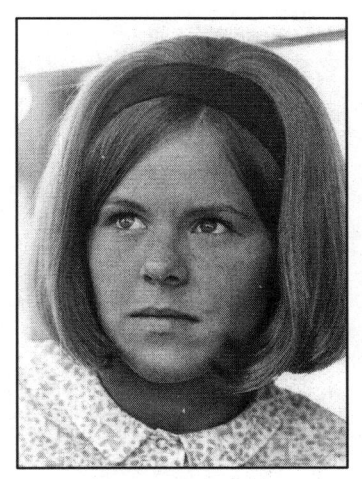

Janet

as fast. So we sped to Bozeman where the ER doctors said she had a 50:50 chance of making it. Had we waited a few more hours, she would have died.

151

You know, I've always believed in Christ and the Holy Spirit, and recently I asked Janet if she remembered being in the Bozeman hospital after that accident. She had a grand mal seizure the day after surgery. When we came in, she was lying curled in bed with her face toward the window and her head swathed in thick bandages. I went behind her and took her bandaged head in my hands, and prayed to the Holy Spirit to heal her and make her well again. She still remembers feeling the healing warmth of my hands around her head.

Looking back, that resort doctor gave us stupid advice and I was angry with him for many years. This was one more time I felt an unseen protection.

What might young graduates learn from my life? I would like them to remember:

- Absorb the value of a penny
- Build integrity by keeping promises
- Get the most education possible
- Persevere; never give up
- Learn by doing what you lack background for
- Ask questions of others to learn from them.
- Do the job you see needs to be done and ask permission later
- Know who can help you do your job
- Take care of yourself so you can care for others
- Make a difference by helping others
- Express your love to and for family and friends
- Develop an attitude of thankfulness for blessings

How much success have I had throughout my life? Whether in the business world or my private life, I think some. I know I am loved and dear friends, like Jim Sayles, the Morettis and my caretaking angel Danielle, know I love them. My beloved wife is a treasure to both our children and me. This is my daughter's poem, framed in our home:

The Majic Lies Within

Come with me and see,
all the wonders to behold.
Within you lies the key
to unlock the door to me.
Quietly within, you can hear
my voice unfold.
You need only to believe,
and my treasures you'll perceive.
My love engulfs thy temple
in all that you do.
Never will I forsake you,
this you should know to be true.
Be aware and know that
I am everywhere

Know that I have always been,
and will forever be, a part
of your soul for all eternity.
— *J. Bond*
June 21, 1992

I don't know how it could get any better.

Looking Back

Joe H and Jim Sayles

Walleye caught from Lake Ontario by Joe H, far left, Jerry Carlson (no hat) middle, Ed Knighton, his three sons and guide

Somebody's Watching Over Me

HAPPY BIRTHDAY

THE BEST DAD IN
    THE WORLD

Some Dad's are skinny, some are fat.

Others are dull, exciting, or full of gull.

One may have red hair, brown, or grey.

But mine is most perfect and the best in everyway.

Love
Jan

My Dad

When we come into this world we are blessed with two angelic guides in physical form, a Mother and a Father. I have been blessed many times over with the parents I am fortunate to have. My Dad has been the foundation of our family and the essence of family that exudes from my Dad is LOVE. There are many words to describe my Dad but this sentence captures the spirit of my Dad.

A helpful, loving, caring, spiritual man, who is tenacious and perseveres confidently with courage, faith, and dignity as he flows through this experience we call life.

My Dad is also a teacher in so many ways, impacting the lives of individuals in positive, profound ways. I am so grateful for the wisdom of spirituality that my Dad has shared and passed on, not only to me, but my children and those extended lives that he has touched. Truth be told, as children we were aware of the "Secret" long ago because of the teachings Dad communicated to us. I know I consider myself extremely lucky and grateful that God has used you as an instrument to spread His divine Love Dad. Your entire family has benefited from your love, wisdom, and humility in so many ways that thank you just does not seem adequate.

Although, there are times we wish Dad wasn't so tenacious because when he gets something in his mind, by gosh he doesn't let it go until he witnesses results and positive results at that. Mom and I always joke that we are going to have a caricature done of Dad as a bulldog with a bone in his mouth. To your credit, that tenacity as served you well Dad! My Dad has always been my rock of Gibraltar and one of my biggest cheerleaders.

From the time my brothers and I were little, education has always been something that Dad has encouraged us to strive for. Between you and me Dad the encouragement was sometimes a little tough and you know what I mean. But as I became older, one thing Dad always told us is that "your education is an invisible gold bracelet that you earned and no one can ever take away from you." Thank you for all your encouragement and support.

Dad, I am so lucky to have you for my Father, words cannot do justice to express my appreciation for all you have done for me, the support you have given me, the things that you have taught me, and the love that you show me in all that you do.

You truly are my Hero Dad and
I Love You Very Much!

Looking Back

From My Heart to Your Heart,
My Soul to Your Soul

— Your One and Only Daughter, 2007

For My Dad

The cycle of life . . . infinite and eternal . . . now is the time to reflect on what my Father meant to me and how he influenced my life in so many positive ways. I am thankful to have chosen Joseph H. Wessels as my Father, my Mentor, and my Friend.

This relationship blossomed on April 17, 1958, when I was born. Now at age 49, close to when we shall part ways, but only for a moment in time. Certainly my faith tells me we will be together again.

As a Father the most important thing my Dad demonstrated to me early in life was the love for my Mother, his wife and eternal soul mate. He has always acted respectfully and appreciative of his family. Dad was willing and eager to support, provide, and protect his family in any situation. He never backed down on what he felt was proper, honest, and worthy. A true fighter, a man who had backbone and was a defender of morality. He lived the truest of lives and showed me unconditional love.

He was a Father who lived to support, encourage, understand and communicate the belief and lifestyle of his family. One who "always" wanted things to go the best, he had a drive to give, give, give — surely an understatement when it came to his work ethic. Dad was a man of his word, one we could all count on. His athletic commitment throughout his life was a true indication that he truly believed in "no pain, no gain."

A veteran of World War II, he served in the Third Cavalry ("Brave Rifles") under Patton's Ghost Troops. He received medals for Good Conduct, the American Campaign, the European Campaign, World War II Victory, for being a Sharp Shooter of which he was the most proud, and Honorable Service. Among the first to liberate the concentration camps in Europe, he possessed courage and was there when the masses of persecuted humans needed men like himself the most.

My Dad was educated, a Wayne State University graduate, a follower and teacher of Coptic philosophy. He was a man of faith believing and living the light and love of the Holy Spirit. He is and was respected by the family and his friends. Because of these fine exceptional characteristics, my Father became a self-made man in every respect, a wonderful man whom I love for all he has taught me, like learning to meditate, evolving to a higher plain and the lessons of karma. You taught me good, sometimes I didn't listen.

In closing, my Dad is my best friend, one who understands me for myself and loves me for who I am. I love him for who he was and will continue to be in the light and love of the Holy Spirit. I'm sure we will be together again and that we will all be at peace and comforted with that faith. Until then,

I Love You Now and Always, Dad

— Your son, Steve, 2007

My Father

I was asked to write a little something about my Father. I would like to write about both my Father and Mother. This is not a small or minor endeavor. In fact, there is nothing neither small nor minor about my parents. The man is inspirationally larger than life itself and my Mother is the most loving supportive woman that a Father with a family needs.

The ideals and concepts of life imparted to me through a kind, inspiriting and nurturing way have manifested visualizations in my mind's eye and defined me the way I am today. I hope to also nurture and inspire my children in the same fashion.

Love of God and Country, Dedication to Family, Courage, Honor, Honesty, Respect for Others, Self Respect, Self Reliance, Faith, Hope, Trust, Spirituality, Wisdom and Insight are just a short list of the ideals and concepts that my Father and Mother have endowed my life. Others should be so lucky.

I Remember When

- In the first grade I slipped in the mud and heard Ms. Huffty would put a dress on boys who got their pants wet. I called home from the principal's office, and Mom was shopping—not available to bring me a change of clothes—so I packed up my stuff and walked home. The school principal and others called the house, looking for me. No answer from me, and no dress. Mom, thanks for not taking me back there that day. After all, I was not going to wear a dress for anyone.
- I was a pain in the ass in fifth grade. I got spanked for not doing my homework. While in the exclusion room, melting crayons on the

Looking Back

heating unit, shooting paper spit wads at a BB hole in the window, hoping to get a hole-in-one, when I was supposed to write 500 times how much I should pay attention to and appreciate suckie art pictures. Father and Mother were baffled and didn't know what to do, but were there to support me no matter what.

- I was in Boy Scouts on a camping trip, and we had to sleep on the ground in tents. It was rainy and cold. My Father was with me, although he did not like the situation, as he did his time in WWII with worse conditions, but my Father was there.

- I played sports in high school: football, baseball and wrestling. God forbid I should get hurt. Father and Mother attended my events and were there to support me with words of encouragement.

- My first year of college at Olivet was a blur of learning, hunting and sports. Father and Mother were excited for me, but not sure if I was somehow dropped on my head, looking at each other, not knowing who was responsible for my immaturity and inevitable demise. Still, my Father and Mother gave me words of encouragement and support.

- I transferred to Western Michigan University for the remainder of my college career and got more serious about education. I held two jobs and went to school and played one season of semi-pro football. Father and Mother were supportive, but I made them a nervous wreck with the football thing because I had no insurance. God forbid I should get hurt. They were still supportive.

- After graduation I continued to work for Tru-Green Lawn Care. They sent me to Pittsburgh, Virginia Beach and Tampa. I was desperate for a real job. Got a call from Parker-Hannifin, and I'm sure my Father had something to do with the offer, but flew to Chicago and got the job as a Territory Manager. Thank you, Dad! After the training I received from my Father, I did well for them. Jim Hanus called me the "executive with rough edges," and I received many awards for performance.

- After Parker, I took a job with DePatie Fluid Power. My Father was a mentor of inspiration to technology. I was a neophyte to the technology available. After exposure to the automation technology available in industry, I became driven to accomplish more than my Father ever dreamed.

- I am now a respected Manager/Supervisor/Planner/Scheduler in the nuclear power generation industry.

Looking Back

    There are numerous examples of my Father's love and inspiration not provided in this short essay, as my fingers are tired, but my heart, mind and tongue are not. Ask me. I will try to share the ideas and concepts that are his and God's to share.

    Love of God and Country, Dedication to Family, Courage, Honor, Honesty, Respect for Others, Self Respect, Self Reliance, Faith, Hope, Trust, Spirituality, Wisdom and Insight. These are the things that make the difference and good people. I thank God that I had a Dad and Mom that gave these ideas to me.

    Love You Both Eternally,

— Joe C, 2007

ADDITIONS & CORRECTIONS

p.99, line 10, . . . our Lakeway house,

p.99, line 15, . . . moved to Stone Henge

p.90, line 1, . . . Depatie Fluid Dynamics never existed.

p.95, line 2, . . . Carl Moretti, Jim Curtis, and Joe Meliwiki.

p.95, line 3, . . . Jim Chambers is still going strong with his company, Fluid Connections, Inc.

p.95, line 7, . . . Our company, Depatie Fluid Power, prospered.

p.140, lines 17–18, . . . Tuesday evenings in 1969 to listen to Master Stanley lecture on the Coptic philosophy.

Index inserts

    Bond, Janet Wessels (daughter)
        tribute by, 156A–156C
    Coptic philosophy, 138, 140, 148
    Curtis, Jim, 95
    Depatie Fluid Power, 92, 95, 148
    Fluid Connections, Grand Rapids, 93, 95
    Lakeway Avenue home, 96–97, 99
    Stanley, Master, 140
    Wessels, Joseph C. (son, "Joey")
        tribute by, 156E–156I
    Wessels, Steve (son)
        essay by, 148–149, 156C–156E

Index

A

Agnew, Mich., xii, 1
Alpena, Mich., trip to, 146
American Indian friend, impact of, 5–7
Andrews, Mr. (son's teacher), 148
Arab customs, 103
Austria, World War II, 48, 49–60, 56, 62
  map, 50

B

Baja California, Mexico, 144
Bereavement training, 123
Bethke, Ella (aunt), 2, 137
Bethke, Marie (aunt), 2
Bethke, Theodore and Augusta (grandparents), 1–2, 20
Bethke, Walter (uncle), 2
Bimini, Bahamas, trip to, 146
Blessings, 99, 109, 136, 140, 142
Bombers (aircraft), 43, 71
Bond, Dick, 130–131
Bond, Janet Wessels (daughter), 79, 89
  horseback riding accident, 150–152
  poems by, 154, 156
Bosnia, inhumanity in, 59
Boyne Citizen (newspaper), 24–25
Boyne City, Mich., xii, 15, 25, 136
  Aunt Ella in, 2
  moves to or from, 4, 19, 23, 128
B&P (Brooks & Perkins), Detroit, 70–72, 76, 79
"Brave Rifles," 33, 49, 52
Brave Rifles Bugle (newsletter), 49, 59
Brennan, Captain, 51–52, 55–56
Bronson Care Center, Vicksburg, 119

Bronson Place, Kalamazoo, 121
Brooks & Perkins ("B&P"), Detroit, 70–72, 76, 79
Buck, Billy, 55

C

Camp Gordon, Georgia, 32, 33
Camp Grant, Illinois, 64
Camp Lucky Strike, LeHarve, 63
Camp Schanks, New York, 40
Canada trips, 145, 146–147
Carlson, Jerry, 155
Catholics vs. Protestants as Christians, 104
Cavalry, U.S. history and, 33–34, 60
Chambers, Jim, 93–95
Checker Cab Co., driving for, 66–69, 76
Cherbourg Beach, France, 44, 45–46
Chevrolet, sales competition with, 83
China trip, 105
Christ. See Jesus Christ
Christians
    behaviorial, 104, 143
    Catholics vs. Protestants as, 104
    Episcopalians, 112, 136–137
Christmas gifts, 2, 5–6, 18, 20, 137
Coptic philosophy, 138, 148
Cousin Earl, 3, 16
Cousin Frank, 3, 16

Cow stories, 11–13
Cricken, Michael, 37

D

Deaths, 14–15, 104, 143
    concentration camp inmates, 49, 53–54
    hospice patients, 116, 122, 123
Depatie, Diane (niece), 145
Depatie, Frank, 89, 92, 94
Depatie, Frank and Todd, family, 145
Depatie, Kim (niece), 145
Depatie, Michael (nephew), 145
    wife Holly and, 129–130
Depatie, Todd Street, 145
Depatie Fluid Dynamics, 95
Depatie Fluid Power, 92, 148
Detroit, Mich., 79
    dating in, 76–78
    jobs in, 66, 70, 80
Dilworth Hotel, Boyne City, 136
Direct Credits Society, 137
Discourses (John-Roger), 141

E

Ebensee (concentration camp), Austria, 49–60
    barracks, 54
    crematory area, 53–55, 57
    infirmary, 53
    liberation of, 49, 52–53, 55–57
Egypt trip, 100
Emotional Manifestation (Lawson), 138

Index

England, transport to, 43–44
Ethnic heritage, 1–2, 3
European combat, World War II
   London bombardment, 43–44
   Third Cavalry in, 46–48, 60–62
   training for, 34–35

F
Family trips, 145–146, 149
"Father" (S. Wessels), 148–149
Finnish descent, 118
Fishing trips, 144, 146–147, 149, 155
Fleming, Tech.Sgt. Kansas, 42
Florida trips, 145
Fluid Connections, Grand Rapids, 93
Ford, Mr. Henry II, 88
Ford coupe, 19–20
Ford Crest News, circulation, 84
Ford Motor Company, working for, 80, 82–89, 91
   editor, 84
   market analyses, 84
   sales promotion and training, 83, 85–88
France, World War II
   Cherbourg Beach, 44, 45–46
   LeHarve, 62–63
   U.S. cavalry campaign in, 46–48

G
Gabriel (archangel), and The Prophet, 102–103
German ancestry, 1–2
Germany, World War II, 35, 48
Gifts
   bicycle as, 21
   Christmas and, 2, 5–6, 20
   farewell, 71, 91–92
God
   blessings from, 99, 142
   cross-cultural belief in, 101, 136
   nature of, 139, 143
   prayers to, 59, 137
"God bless America" (song), 109
Golden Rule, 59
Golf, 96, 111, 115, 124
   caddying for, 24, 27
   as fundraisers, 125
Goodell School, Lincoln Park, 4
Grand Haven, Mich., xii, 1, 19, 20–21
Great Depression, 4
   improvement organizations during, 137
   struggle during, 11–20, 135–136
Gun Lake, Mich., party, 107

H
Hamdy, Aziz
   friendship with, 100–101
   Muslim studies with, 102–103
   preparation for burial, 104

Hamdy, Heide, 100–102
Harbor Springs, Mich., trips to, 145
Hidden Cover home, Kalamazoo, 99
H.M.S. Synthia, 43
Holiday Lane home, Kalamazoo, 98–99
Holt, Father James, 112
Hospice Care of Southwest Michigan, xi
Hospice volunteer, 112
   client stories, 113–128
      "90-year old," 127–128
      "Anch," 117–123
      "David, 18-year old," 114–116
      "Earl," 124–125
      "John," 116–117
      "Win by Losing," 113–114
   jobs as, 122, 123, 124, 125
   purposes, 112–113, 125
   residential facilities, 126–127 (*see also* Rose Arbor Hospice)
Hunting trips, 146, 149

I

Iacocca, Lee, 88
Inhumanity, 58–59
Ireland, Christian religious terrorism in, 104

J

Japan, World War II, 62, 65–66

Jesus Christ
   Holy Spirit of, 140, 152
   as spiritual leader, 104, 143
   teachings of, 138, 140
John-Roger, MISA and, 139, 140–142

K

Kalamazoo, Mich.
   homes in, 92, 95–99
   jobs in, 89, 92–98
Kalamazoo Country Club, 115
Knighton, Dr. Ed, 155
Kokomo, Indiana, xii, 3
Kosovo, inhumanity in, 59

L

Lake Charlevoix, 5
Lake Michigan, 21
Lakeway Avenue home, 96–97
Latiolais, Laura, xi
Lawson, Alfred, books and teachings of, 137–138
Lincoln Park, Mich., xii, 3–4
Living well, dying well: stories from Rose Arbor Hospice (Murphy), xi, 114
London bombardment, 43–44
Lucky (dog), 10
Luxembourg, World War 11, 48

M

"Majic lies within, The" (J. Bond), 154

Index

Mazur, Ed, 51–52, 53, 55
Melwiki, Joe, 95, 122–123
Mental Manifestation
    (Lawson), 138
Mentees and mentors
    Derk, 129–130
    Dick Bond, 130–131
    Mr. Sayles, 28, 75, 76
Michigan State University, 129
Milham Golf Course, 96
Miller-Davis Co., 98
Milwood Apartments, 97–98
MISA (Movement of Spiritual
    Inner Awareness),
    138–139, 140–142
Montana trips, 150–152
Moretti, Carl, 95
Moretti, Carl and Pat, 106–109, 153
Moretti, Missy, 108–109
Morton, John, 139
Moses, as spiritual leader, 104
Movement of Spiritual Inner
    Awareness (MISA),
    138–139, 140–142
    booklets and tapes for
        initiates, 141–142
Movies, 14, 25, 80
Murphy, Brenda Fettig, xi
Muslim friends, 100–104
Muslim studies, with Aziz
    Hamdy, 102–103

N
New York City, 40, 65
NuCon Systems, 92–93

O
Onyx (dog), 146
Oval Beach, 21

P
Packard Motor Car Co., 76
Paper mill layoffs, Kalamazoo, 2
Patton, General George S., Jr., 34, 46, 61–62
Peake, Dr., 100
Perkins, Mr. ("B&P" owner), 71–72
Persinger, Bob, 52, 55
Physical Manifestation
    (Lawson), 138
Pneumatic control companies, 92–93
Pomante, Dick, 52, 55
Portage Northern (high
    school), 129
Prayers, 59, 137, 152
Prophet, The
    archangel Gabriel and, 102–103
    as spiritual leader, 103–104
Protestants *vs.* Catholics as
    Christians, 104
Public Works Administration, 18
Purple Gang, 4

Q
Qu'ran studies, 102–103

R
Religious terrorism, 104

Roosevelt, President Franklin D., 17–18
Rose Arbor Hospice, xi, 110, 127
Rykse's Restaurant, Kalamazoo, 123

S

St. Luke's Episcopal Church, Kalamazoo, 111–112
St. Paul's Episcopal Cathedral, Detroit, 78–79, 136
Sanders, Danielle, 108, 131–132, 153
Sayles, Jim, 14, 23, 26, 75–76, 77, 153, 155
Sayles, Mr. (mentor), 28, 75, 76
Sayles, Robert ("Bob"), 14, 24, 77
Scott, William C. ("Bill"), 84, 87–88
Scott, General Winfield, 33
Sheep stories, 7–8, 16, 103
Skiing trips, 149
Soul, nature of God and, 139, 143
Spanish ancestry, 3
Spiritual energy, 138, 140, 152
Sponsel, Clif, 70–71
Stanley, Watson W., 40–41, 49–50, 59, 62
Steyr, Austria, 60
Stonehenge home, Kalamazoo, 99

T

Tax write-offs, 96

Thomas, John, 95
Top Hatters, Ford Division, 86
Trips
 Dorothy and Joe, 100, 105, 121
 family, 145–146, 149, 150–152
 fishing, 144, 146–147, 149, 155
 hunting, 146, 149
 skiing, 149
Truck Sales Workshop, 85, 87–88, 91

U

U.S. Army, World War II, 66
 basic training, 34–40
 deployment, 42–43
 draftee, 4, 33
 European experience, 43–62
 furloughs, 40, 65
 jobs in, 34, 38–40
 maneuvers, 35–37, 40
 pay rates, 37–38
 provisions, 36–37, 44–45, 46–47
 reunions, 52, 121
 Third Cavalry, 33–34, 47–48, 49, 60
U.P. (Upper Peninsula), Michigan, xii, 118, 119

V

Van Houten, Beth Carroll, 113
Vegetarians, 148–149
Vienna, Austria, warehouses, 56

Index

Vogel, Charlie, 72
Volunteer in retirement. *See* Hospice volunteer

W

Wainwright, Colonel Jonathan M., 34
Wakefield, Sergeant, 51
Walloon Lake, 6
Walloon Lake Country Club, 24, 26–28
War, personal impact of, 47, 59, 130–131
 See also World War II
Wayne State University, 58, 79–80
Weapons, 27, 48
Wessel boys, 21
Wessels, Amanda (granddaughter), ix–x
Wessels, Bert (uncle), 3
Wessels, Darwin (cousin), 3
Wessels, Dorothy Street (wife)
 courtship, 76–78, 136
 marriage and family, 79–80, 89, 95–96, 99, 121, 143, 154
 photographs, iv, 74, 78, 107
 as volunteer, 111–112, 120
Wessels, Emma Marie Bethke (mother), 1
 Great Depression and, 11–14, 15, 17, 19
 occupations, 18, 23, 136
 siblings, 2
Wessels, Ettie (aunt), 3, 16
Wessels, Glenn (cousin), 3
Wessels, Joseph C. (son, "Joey"), 79, 89
 rescues and, 97–98, 150
Wessels, Joseph Henry (grandfather), 1, 3, 5, 7
 death of, 14–15
 home in Boyne City, 4, 10
Wessels, Joseph Henry ("Joe"), 1924–
 awards, 23–24, 39, 40, 47–48
 birthdays, 1, 132, 156
 education, 4, 18, 21, 28, 30, 58, 79–80, 102–103
 family
  children (*see* Bond, Janet Wessels; Wessels, Joseph C.; Wessels, Steve)
  cousins, 3, 16
  grandchildren, ix–x, 79
  grandparents, 1–2, 3
  great-grandparents, 3
  parents, 1, 2, 3, 17, 19, 65
  siblings (*see* Wessels, Joy)
  wife (*see* Wessels, Dorothy Street)
 interests, 149
 legacies, 152–154
 military service (*see* U.S. Army)

163

Wessels, Joseph Henry ("Joe"), 1924–, *cont.*
   photographs, iv, 3, 10, 30, 32, 38, 39, 42, 48, 62, 78, 107, 132, 144, 155
   post-war jobs, 66, 70, 80, 90, 142, 148
   pre-war jobs, 22, 24–28, 29–31, 136
   retirement, 111, 124, 128, 131 (*see also* Hospice volunteer)
   spiritual beliefs, 136, 138–142
Wessels, Joseph William (father), 1, 3, 27
   health, 23, 76, 136
   occupations, 4, 5, 7, 15–16, 18–19, 76
   reading requirements from, 137
Wessels, Joy (sister), 2, 3, 5, 14, 20, 24, 65
Wessels, Sarah (great-grandmother), 3, 21
Wessels, Steve (son), ix, 79, 89, 147
   dating by, 129, 150
   daughter, ix–x
   essay by, 148–149

West Michigan Hydraulics, 93, 94
World War II
   Austria to France in, 62
   cavalry in, 33, 34, 47
   England to France in, 43–46
   European combat in, 46–48
   Japan and, 61, 65–66
   liberation of concentration camp, 49–60

X
Xian, China, terra cotta soldiers near, 105–106

Y
"You were there" (A. Wessels), x

Z
Zement. *See* Ebensee (concentration camp), Austria
Zimmerman, Frank, 88, 91–92